VINCENZO
VENEZIA

anxious preoccupied attachment

Break the Cycle of Anxiety, Looming Fear of Abandonment and Grow a Deeper Connection with Your Partner Without Feeling Unworthy of Love

ISBN: 979-12-81498-19-8

TABLE OF CONTENTS

INTRODUCTION

As we live in a society where images of love and relationships are constantly presented, it is not surprising that most of us are in some way concerned with performing and creating relationships. You might think you must be in a strong, exclusive relationship to feel loved, accepted, and fulfilled. But the very things that fill your heart with joy and love simultaneously fill you with fear and anxiety. The traits that make you feel so lovable also cause you to become insecure and question your self-worth. You want to feel loved and accepted, but you also want to be independent and self-sufficient. And you don't want to be alone, but you can't stand the demands of being in a relationship.

The reality is that how our parents or caregiver loved us when we were young has a lifelong effect on our mental health and how we handle relationships in adulthood. Our mothers or caregivers made us feel loved, secure, ignored, rejected, and ashamed. From the moment you are born, the people in your environment set the stage for your emotional availability or lack thereof. Many of us are unconsciously carrying this emotional baggage from childhood into adulthood.

As you grow up and attempt to figure out what love and intimacy are all about, you are faced with the dilemma of wanting to feel loved and accepted but not wanting to be controlled or hurt by a relationship. The fear and anxiety you experience as a child enters your adult relationships, creating an anxious preoccupied attachment style.

Nevertheless, you need to understand that it's not your fault. It's not that your parents or caregiver did anything wrong. It's hard to say whether you would have turned out the same way if they had been a little more loving and consistent with you as a child. You were raised in a certain way and had issues to work through before you could begin learning healthy relationship skills.

This book aims to offer you the most practical information about anxious attachment and how to cultivate a secure attachment style. This book will also teach you how to overcome relationship anxieties, what attachment is, and how it affects your life from an emotional standpoint. You will become more aware and learn the difference between healthy and unhealthy anxiety. You will also gain the tools you need to manage those anxieties, so they do not negatively affect your relationship.

The good news is you do not have to be anxious about your ability to connect with another human being. You do not need to avoid love and relationships because it does not imply that you are weak or that you cannot or will not be loved and accepted. Love and relationships are often associated with suffering and loss because we all have to go through difficult times, disappointments, and heartbreak. However, you do not need to live in fear of being hurt by a relationship or a person. It is the most hopeful sign if you are having a hard time in relationships because it means you are aware that something is not right and are open to change.

You can have an enjoyable relationship that makes you happy and feel loved without the fear of being controlled or trapped. You can have the feeling of security in a relationship without having to feel ashamed or guilty. You can learn to communicate well and feel loved and accepted in your relationships. You do not need to be one way or the other; however, if you are anxious in relationships, this book will teach you how to let go of that anxiety so that you can have close relationships and make yourself happy.

PART 1

WHAT IS ANXIOUS PREOCCUPIED ATTACHMENT?

CHAPTER 1

WHAT IS ATTACHMENT

Attachment is how an individual sees themselves, their needs and wants, and their sense of self and identity about others. It is how we form connections with others and see ourselves in those connections. We perceive the world, our place in it, and our relationships through it.

JOHN BOWLBY ATTACHMENT THEORY

John Bowlby is one of the founders of attachment theory and is regarded as the father of this field. His theories and observations became the basis for further studies regarding how we relate to others depending on our past experiences, especially with our primary caregivers.

A part of Bowlby's theory is that humans are naturally wired for "intimacy." By this, he means that we biologically develop from birth with a desire to form close bonds with others. The attachment system is a basic emotion-driven behavioral system that directs an infant or child to seek proximity to their caregiver when in distress and to maintain contact during moments of comfort and security. The attachment system stays with us well into adulthood and sets the framework for forming relationships and our expectations of others.

Bowlby also relates the concept of attachment to evolution, saying that attachment is a survival mechanism that our ancestors put in place for their offspring to ensure their security and survival. Incidentally, Bowlby also thought of attachment as a goal-corrected partnership. This means that a child's attachment to their caregivers is rooted in the satisfaction of the caregiver's needs, which helps guide the child towards that satisfaction. In essence, attachment provides a mutual benefit, further strengthening the bond between caregiver and child.

Bowlby's theories on attachment stem from his observations of children who were separated from their primary caregiver at an early age, either for adoption or by the caregiver's death. He studied how they coped and adapted to their new environment. He also observed children who experienced an absent caregiver, such as a parent frequently away for work or another reason. In all his observations, Bowlby noticed that the most important element for the child in adapting to their new environment was the child-caregiver relationship and attachment.

As described in his book, *Attachment and Loss*, Bowlby concludes that the child forms a mental representation of the primary caregiver early in life, which he calls "internal working models." This internal representation of the primary caregiver becomes the child's template for forming relationships and expecting others to behave.

These internal representations are created when a child experiences their first relationship with another person. This relationship establishes a pattern of relating that can last a lifetime and make up the core belief system. In this mental representation, the child establishes comfort, security, love, and how to expect someone to behave with them.

Critical Period for Developing an Attachment

Bowlby proposes that there is a critical period for attachment development. The term is most frequently encountered in the study of imprinting, where it is believed that young birds can only form a bond with their mother during a specific period shortly after hatching. These factors affect the maturation of processes, including hearing and vision, social bonding, and language acquisition. Suppose a person is not exposed to the stimuli required to learn a skill during a critical stage of its development. In that case, it may be difficult or even impossible for them to develop certain functions related to that ability later in life.

Neurologically, critical periods are characterized by high levels of brain plasticity before neural connections become increasingly stable. Specifically, critical periods tend to conclude when GABA-inhibiting synapses reach maturity, which can be accelerated by adult signaling of the neural circuitry.

As brains develop, their connections become more stable. The transitions of the brain from a more plastic to a more fixed state allow it to advantageously retain new and complex processes, such as perceptual, motor, and cognitive functions. However, if the brain is exposed to too much stress or experiences loss at a young age, it can put itself into an unadaptive "stuck" state. This can lead to greater difficulties in adulthood, including anxiety and self-destructive behavior. Attachment figures play a vital role in developing one's neurobiological processes and are critical for healthy development.

Children's gestures, such as pride, predict how they will acquire oral language skills, which are crucial for developing executive functions. However, the formation of stable connections in the brain can limit future revisions to the brain's neural circuitry. For instance, if a young organism undergoes abnormal sensory experiences, such as auditory or visual deprivation, during the critical period, the brain may not properly wire itself to process future sensory inputs.

The following are ages and their needed developmental and emotional experiences:

a. 0-2.5 years: "pre-attachment phase"

The child is just beginning to form their internal working model, which includes the attachment template and general expectations about how parents/caregivers behave in the world. The child has not directly experienced enough to know how their parents/caregivers will respond, so they form a general expectation of behavior and then observe the caregiver's response to that behavior.

If the caregiver responds to the children's expectations, this will strengthen their working model. If the caregiver does not respond in accordance with their expectations or ignores them as if they are of no importance, this will undermine and destabilize their working model.

During this phase, if children feel that they must be vigilant about seeking out connections with their caregiver, that is a stressor. This will result in the emergence of a state of hypervigilance, which will make children feel even more insecure when they are in the proximity of their caregiver. They may also develop anxiety and startle easily, so they will be more likely to become fearful or withdraw from others to cope with their stress.

b. 2.5-7 years: the "proto-attachment" phase

This is when a child begins to understand the concept of a primary caregiver. The child becomes attached to their primary caregivers and actively seeks their attention, which is seen as a way to establish their needs and security with their caregiver. The attachment process is strengthened by frequent interactions with the primary caregiver, which helps prevent attachment disruptions and maintains the child's expectations of how someone should act towards them consistently. This consistency gives rise to trust and a sense of security in children, which is the foundation for future relationships.

This phase is also characterized by a child's increasing ability to regulate their own emotions and learn how to self-soothe. They also begin to understand their need to feel safe and comfortable with others. This gives the child trust and security, setting their expectations for future relationships. These expectations include delivering comfort when experiencing negative emotions as well as being able to give comfort when needed.

A lack of trust and dependence on others can develop when a child experiences numerous disruptions in their caregiving relationship. These disruptions could include the absence of their primary caregiver, the loss of someone close to them, or the lack of consistency in how their caregivers act with them. This leads to mistrust and uncertainty because a child cannot rely on others for support and, therefore, must learn to support themselves. When a child is not able to bond with their primary caregiver, they often turn to other sources of comfort, such as pets, objects, or other children. They also have difficulty interpreting people's intentions and feelings towards them as they cannot understand the concept of loyalty or connection in relationships. This can lead to uncertainty and mistrust in interpersonal relationships throughout life.

c. 7-12 years: the "latency phase."

This period is characterized by the child engaging in numerous exploratory activities while developing their cognitive abilities and physical skills. They also reach a basic understanding of how the world works and become increasingly independent.

During this phase, a child is still dependent on their primary caregivers. As they learn to communicate their needs and expectations and receive the appropriate support from them, the child will develop better self-confidence and a stronger identity. They will also better understand their needs and the ability to self-soothe themselves. This further helps them understand their role in relationships and how to support others. During this time, individuals develop their interests and hobbies and interact socially with others in groups.

A lack of trust is experienced when a child experiences frequent disruptions in the caregiving relationship, leading to mistrust and uncertainty because they cannot rely on their primary caregivers for emotional support. The result is that they cannot understand the concept of loyalty or connection in relationships, which leads them to lack trust in many areas of life. They also have difficulty interpreting people's intentions and feelings towards them as they cannot understand the concept of loyalty or connection in relationships, which leads them to lack trust in many areas of life.

d. 12-18 years: the "adolescent phase."

This is characterized by the child beginning to develop their identity, social, and personal skills, and by their separation from their primary caregivers. They begin to interact with others based on their common interests instead of for survival or protection. During this phase, teenagers develop a more mature concept of attachment which helps them cope with new situations that involve critical relationships and the separation or loss of their primary caregiver.

In adolescence, a child begins to separate from their parents and form their own independent identity. Although they still rely on the support of their primary caregivers, the child is gaining a better understanding of how to interact with others based on common interests and how to reciprocally give support when needed. This further helps them develop self-confidence, assertiveness, and independence in relationships. It also allows them to draw on past experiences to understand what they need in other relationships that encourage closeness and comfort.

A lack of consistency in the relationship between a child and their primary caregiver can lead to an increased breakdown in communication and can cause a child to experience more distrust. This results in a lack of understanding of loyalty in relationships and all the difficulties that come with it, such as a lack of trust, a greater misinterpreting of intentions, and expectations that are not met.

The disruption in a caregiving relationship can affect attachment functions later in life. The "security" developed throughout the early years is crucial for how people function later. What the child experiences during this period directly affects their perception of others, affecting adult relationships.

CHAPTER 2

WHAT IS ANXIOUS PREOCCUPIED ATTACHMENT

Anxious preoccupied attachment is one of the attachment styles described by John Bowlby's attachment theory. An anxious-preoccupied attachment style is a form of adult attachment (also called ambivalent when referring to infant attachment). It is one of the three insecure attachment styles characterized by a negative self-perception and a positive image of others.

WHAT CAUSES ANXIOUS PREOCCUPIED ATTACHMENT

Attachment styles can change, and that also includes anxious preoccupied attachment. While it may sometimes be clear why someone may develop this type of attachment style, there are certain situations in which it is much easier for it to come about.

Some of the reasons why people develop anxious preoccupied attachments are as follows:

1. Genetics

It has been found that some people are naturally predisposed to developing an anxious-preoccupied attachment style because of their genetics. This is because there is evidence showing that anxious-attachment patterns can be inherited or passed down through generations in families through genetic material (e.g., DNA) that is passed from one generation to the next. This is done through a process called epigenetic changes that can impact the function of genes through changes in cell structure and gene expression. Therefore, if a person has an anxious-attachment style early on in life, there is a greater chance that they will continue to develop it (i.e., the anxious-preoccupied pattern) throughout their lifetime.

A genetic component predicts how a child will develop attachment styles regardless of other environmental factors and parental behaviors (i.e., insecure vs. secure attachment). Grossman et al. (1998) found a significant relationship between genetics and attachment styles: 48% of the variance in attachment styles can be explained by genetic factors, while non-genetic factors can explain only 24%. As such, researchers have begun to explore what genes are involved with attachment disorder and anxious-preoccupied attachment style. However, because this field of study is still young, no particular genes have been linked to an anxious-preoccupied attachment style.

In some cases, a child may be naturally predisposed to develop an anxious-preoccupied attachment style (i.e., a genetic predisposition for developing this pattern) due to epigenetic changes in their DNA. This is why studies have been conducted to see if specific genes are associated with an anxious-preoccupied attachment style. A study by Shah and Block (2014) examined the role of serotonin transporter (5-HTT) gene polymorphisms in the development of anxious-preoccupied attachment style by comparing a high-functioning (HFA, anxious-preoccupied and avoidant attachment styles) group of children with a low-functioning (LFA, secure and ambivalent attachment styles) group of children. The results found that children with the HFA gene had significantly higher anxiety levels than those involved in the LFA group. On the other hand, researchers found no significant differences in attachment styles among children involved in the LFA group. This suggests that genetic factors are involved with the anxious-preoccupied attachment style. However, studies have yet to find specific genes associated with this particular type of attachment style.

2. Hormonal factors

Like genetics, hormones and neurotransmitters can also play a significant role in this attachment style. During pregnancy—especially at the end—during birth, and even after birth, there are certain hormonal changes that can affect how we look at others around us and how we connect to them based on our individual needs. Examples of these hormones include oxytocin and cortisol. Oxytocin is the love hormone, or the "attachment" hormone, because it is released during physical contact, like when we hug someone. It helps create a sense of connection to others, which is vital for developing attachment styles, especially anxious-preoccupied.

On the other hand, cortisol is the hormone responsible for our fight-or-flight response and how we react when we are frightened or nervous. Excess cortisol can cause anxiety, panic, and a sense of uneasiness and hypervigilance. All of these are characteristics associated with anxious preoccupied attachment. This is why it is believed that severe trauma during pregnancy, birth, and even after birth may lead to a more anxious-preoccupied attachment style.

Hormonal imbalances can also contribute to this attachment style. For example, suppose the body does not produce enough oxytocin or cortisol (even though some are normal and necessary for survival). In that case, one may be more likely to develop an anxious-preoccupied attachment style as well as other disorders such as depression and anorexia nervosa. This is because they do not receive "enough" hormones and neurotransmitters, which would have led to the development of a secure attachment style.

Anxious-preoccupied attachment is greatly increased (around 160% more) when the mother has migraine headaches during pregnancy. There is evidence showing that oxytocin and cortisol are released when the mother suffers from a migraine. As such, there is reason to believe that if the mother suffers from migraines during pregnancy, it increases an individual's tendency to develop an anxious-preoccupied attachment style later in life.

3. Parenting styles

There are certain parenting styles that can influence whether a child develops anxious preoccupied attachment or not. These include:

a. Authoritarian parenting

Authoritarian parents tend to be controlling; they do not like it if their children do not listen to them and are usually strict and harsh when it comes to discipline and punishment. They also set very high standards for their children and expect them to achieve these high standards easily. Because they have these strict expectations, they often have difficulty accepting their children's shortcomings and faults. This type of parenting style is known to lead to anxious preoccupied attachment. Due to being made to feel accountable for their parents' needs and feelings, these kids experience lifelong guilt.

Authoritarian parents tend to treat their children like they are the parents themselves. As such, the children might think that their opinions don't matter and accept whatever their parents say. It also shows that the child does not have any control over the situation and can be swayed easily by others, especially if they are authoritative figures such as a teacher or a coach.

b. Permissive parenting

A permissive parent is the complete opposite of an authoritarian parent because they are neither strict nor controlling and always let their children have independence and free will (even beyond what is necessary). This can be both beneficial and detrimental to the development of attachment styles and other personality traits later in life. It is bad because it will make the child think that they can get away with anything and have a sense of entitlement due to their parents' lack of control and discipline. However, it could be good if other adults give them proper supervision and guidance outside the home.

This is because they learn more about the outside world through their interactions with people other than just their parents. Having this exposure to people other than their parents also helps them develop a sense of independence, self-reliance, and social skills.

Permissive parents tend to be less serious and more lenient when it comes to discipline and punishment. They also tend to be relaxed and laid back and understand that children are not perfect and make mistakes. As such, they often let their children off the hook without punishing them. They also treat their children as equals, listening to their opinions and taking them into account when making important decisions for the family.

c. Authoritative parenting

Authoritative parents are also strict but do so with a more "loving" and "caring" approach. They believe in a balance between showing their children love and affection while still remaining firm with rules and discipline. They are also open to their children's feelings, desires, and opinions and will have an open dialogue with them to resolve any issues they may have. This type of parenting style will most likely lead to secure attachment in their children as it allows them to express themselves without fear of judgment from their parents.

Authoritative parents are responsive, nurturing, and involved, similar to permissive parents. However, unlike permissive parents, authoritative parents do not excuse their children's bad behavior. Parents with authority take a firm stance and expect their children to behave responsibly and show them proper deference. They also see their children as equal individuals and are willing to discuss an issue with them when they have differing opinions to reach a resolution.

d. Uninvolved parenting

Uninvolved parenting, the opposite of authoritative parenting, is also known as neglectful parenting. It involves not meeting parental responsibilities, such as being a primary parent or disciplining their children. The parents tend to be unconcerned with their children and raise them as if they are not their own. This can be very harmful to their children because they will not be taught important life skills, such as respecting others and behaving in society.

Not only that, but the children will grow up thinking that they are all right not doing anything to help out their parents because, after all, their parents want nothing to do with them. As such, they don't see the point in doing anything productive, such as going to school or helping out around the house. This will lead to the children having low self-esteem and feeling worthless, which can result in them developing anxious-preoccupied attachments as adults.

These four parenting styles (authoritative, authoritarian, permissive, and uninvolved) do play a role in an individual's anxiety-preoccupied attachment. However, it is important to note that they are not necessarily bad or good for everyone, as individuals are truly unique (even if they might seem like they act similarly to each other).

Though not exhaustive, evidence strongly suggests that parenting style affects a child's attachment style. Children who have a secure attachment style are likely to have parents who are authoritative or at least permissive and empathetic towards their children. Children with other attachment styles, such as anxious-ambivalent, avoidant, or disorganized, tend to have authoritarian or permissive parents who do not know how to discipline their children properly and listen to their children's opinions, thoughts, and feelings.

Some research suggests that parenting style can influence an individual's personality. This is because their parents were authoritative or permissive and were effective at expressing high-quality, responsive, and appropriate care or discipline. This would lead to secure attachment (what psychologists refer to as "good" parenting). On the other hand, if their parents were authoritarian or neglectful and did not communicate effectively with them and show support for them (it could be through authoritarian parenting), then secure attachment would be disrupted.

4. Environment

A child's environment can affect their risk of developing anxious-preoccupied attachment. This includes:

a. Peer Group Interactions

Children are more likely to develop anxious-preoccupied attachment if they are in a situation where they are rejected by their peers (i.e., they have no friends). This is because it could make them feel insecure, rejected, and anxious because they see their peers as being more popular and important than them. This would make them feel like outsiders, which could make them more sensitive to rejection. They could become overly dependent on their peers (in hopes of gaining acceptance) and become paranoid about losing the attention of their peers.

b. Societal Stressors

Children who grow up in areas that experience high levels of poverty, crime, and violence tend to have an increased risk of developing anxious-preoccupied attachment. One reason for this is that they may frequently witness violent events, which can make them feel as if they are in constant danger. As such, they will attach themselves to their parents (in hopes of being protected) and be dependent on the decisions their parents make for them. Children who grow up in environments with high levels of stress are also more likely to develop insecure attachment styles. Anxious-preoccupied attachment is likely to be the most common attachment style in these situations because it yields feelings of anxiety and fear towards their social environment (which includes peer groups) as a result of feeling insecure and overwhelmed.

c. Parental Death

Children who lose a parent at an early age (approximately before age 10) have a greater risk of developing an anxious-preoccupied attachment style than adults. This is because they may feel as if they are alone, unloved, and unsupported by their family (which includes friends and other family members). As such, they will develop an anxious-preoccupied attachment style where they want to be close to their peer group because it fills their appetite for love and support (it does not matter whether others reciprocate that love), and they do not want to be alone. They will behave this way because they feel so alone and depend on others for love, making them feel as if they are moving toward their goals (even if short-lived).

This is not to say that children who lose a parent at an early age are necessarily in a high-risk environment. However, they are likely to feel insecure when the loss of a parent occurs and will develop an anxious-preoccupied attachment style.

d. Cultural Factors

Certain cultures may impact the social environment that a child is exposed to and can lead to an anxious-preoccupied attachment style. Asian cultures are very collectivist in nature and place a lot of value on family, school, work, and community over the self. As such, children raised within these cultures tend to have anxious-preoccupied attachment as adults because they have no qualms about being close to their peer group but are very cautious about being close to others outside of these groups (including family members) because they are not necessarily sure of those people's motivations. This is why Asian cultures have a higher prevalence of anxious-preoccupied attachment styles as adults.

This does not mean that only Asian cultures have a higher prevalence of this attachment style, but it is more prevalent in Asian cultures because they are more collectivist in nature. As Western culture becomes more and more globalized, this may also lead to an increased prevalence of anxious-preoccupied attachment styles among adults.

The child's upbringing can significantly influence the development of an anxious-preoccupied attachment style. This attachment style develops as a result of children feeling insecurity, overwhelming loneliness, and an intense desire to be loved. However, this attachment style can also be the result of growing up in certain environments (i.e., a high-stress environment).

5. Neurological Diseases

There are certain neurological diseases that can directly affect a child's ability to develop secure attachment (if they are unable to attach themselves to the caregiver) and can lead to anxious-preoccupied attachment, such as:

a. Autism

Autism is a neurological disorder that affects children's development of attachment and recognition. As a result, many children with autism suffer from insecure attachment. In other words, they develop an anxious-preoccupied attachment style as adults because they do not have the ability to recognize what their caregiver wants them to do or how to interact with them, which makes them feel as if they are being left alone and misunderstood by others.

Autistic children do not develop the ability to understand their caregiver's feelings and may only focus on themselves. As a result, they can easily feel as if they are being smothered and lose their identity over time. This can cause them to have an increased desire to be independent. Alternatively, they may become extremely desperate for affection and try to remain attached to their parents while growing up (to receive love), which can result in an anxious-preoccupied attachment style.

b. Schizophrenia

Schizophrenia is a neurological disease that affects a person's sense of self and others. It can cause difficulties in social relationships, which may also lead to anxious-preoccupied attachment. As with autism, this outcome can occur because the person does not recognize what their caregiver wants them to do (i.e., attach themselves to them) and cannot read others' emotions as well as their own (which could make the person feel like they do not belong in the group), which can lead to them wanting to be close to their peer group for support.

People with schizophrenia attempt to conceal their problems to avoid being judged and out of the fear that others will view them as abnormal due to their own paranoid thoughts (which can make it difficult for them to maintain a secure attachment). However, when they try to achieve social attachment (especially romantic attachments), they feel as if the other person is smothering them because they have so many problems and cannot talk openly about them (to the other person) while they are growing up, which can result in anxious-preoccupied attachment style.

c. Post-Traumatic Stress Disorder

People who develop Post Traumatic Stress Disorder (PTSD) are likely to experience issues with attachment and trust in the future. They may develop an anxious-preoccupied attachment style because they develop signs of depression and dissociation from the traumatic experience. This could make them feel as if others are abandoning them.

They may develop an increased desire to keep their close relationships because they feel insecure about the future. However, it can also lead to a sense of self-blame and shame because they feel as if their behavior has caused their loved ones' abandonment. As a result, these people may try to stay within their relationships or remain attached to them in an attempt to protect themselves from feeling disconnected from others (even though it is not possible). This is why they will likely develop an anxious-preoccupied attachment style as adults so that they do not feel alone and constantly need help from others (even if it is unhealthy) in order to cope with the traumatic situation they have been through.

d. Dissociative Identity Disorder

There are situations where people develop dissociative identity disorder (aka, multiple personality disorder), which could lead to an anxious-preoccupied attachment as adults. Children who experience traumatic events or abuse may develop dissociative identity disorder as a way of coping with the situation at that time. It can also be caused by a traumatic event later in life (such as being in a war).

For example, people who develop dissociation can be "switched" between different personalities when they feel threatened. As anxious-preoccupied attachment is about being overly dependent on others for emotional support, people with this attachment style will often switch between different personalities to deal with their problems.

These people may have one anxious-preoccupied personality, which seeks to stay attached to their loved ones to help them cope with the trauma, often resulting in anxious-preoccupied attachment as adults. This can make them extremely clingy (which can be a negative trait), and they find it difficult to be independent. Alternatively, they may have one or more detached personalities because they feel abandoned by the people they depended on when they were younger (due to their preference to only seek assistance from them). This can also result in an anxious-preoccupied attachment style, as people who are anxious-preoccupied and insecure are more likely to switch between personalities in response to stressful situations.

e. Attention-Deficit Hyperactivity Disorder (ADHD)

People who suffer from attention-deficit hyperactivity disorder (ADHD) are less likely to be able to cope with everyday life because they cannot concentrate properly and get distracted easily in social situations. They may start to feel as if people they know are ignoring them and start to feel anxious, which can prevent them from interacting with others. As a result, they may isolate themselves because of their anxiety and develop an anxious-preoccupied attachment style as adults.

Those who develop basic ADHD in childhood will likely have an anxious-preoccupied attachment style in adulthood because of their poor ability to interact with others and inability to have clear priorities.

f. Depression and Anxiety

People who develop depression or anxiety disorders often feel as if they are afraid of people and withdraw from them (even though it is not a conscious decision). This can lead to anxious-preoccupied attachment because they are constantly worrying about others leaving them (even though it is not possible) and are trying to find ways to fix the situation and make them feel accepted by the people around them.

g. Dyslexia

People with dyslexia have difficulties with auditory and visual perception, which could make it harder for them to understand others' feelings and emotions as well as their own (which can make them feel insecure). They are more likely to develop an anxious-preoccupied attachment style because they are more likely to experience negative emotions when their relationships do not go as planned. This could cause them to seek excessive attention from their loved ones (in an effort to feel secure), which can lead to an anxious-preoccupied attachment style.

h. Borderline Personality Disorder (BPD)

Borderlines have feelings of emptiness and boredom that could lead them to want to attach themselves to others in an attempt to fill that void. They can become excessively dependent on other people for a sense of security. They are more likely to develop an anxious-preoccupied attachment style as adults because they have been rejected or abandoned by their loved ones as children or have witnessed the rejection of their peers, which can make them overly dependent on others.

This is why borderlines may feel smothered by others because they have difficulty expressing their emotional needs in a healthy way, so they become dependent on the relationship for emotional support and intimacy instead. As they are likely to have a long-term relationship with their partner, they will often emphasize the negative traits of their partner in order to make them feel better about themselves (which can be a negative coping strategy). This may lead to anxious-preoccupied attachment as adults.

Cognitive disorders can also affect a person's ability to develop secure attachment because they may not properly understand what their caregiver expects of them (i.e., why the caregiver wants them to attach themselves to them) or correctly identify what the other people in their environment feel and think. As a result, children with cognitive disorders are more likely to develop an anxious-preoccupied attachment style as adults.

6. Other Factors

Other factors can also contribute to the anxious-preoccupied attachment style. These factors are:

a. Sleep Deprivation

Sleep deprivation can lead to an anxious-preoccupied attachment style because it can make people less patient and less aware of the emotional needs of others, and they cannot understand other people's emotions. They are more likely to be anxious, perplexed, and rigid, which makes it challenging for them to relate to and empathize with others.

A study conducted in the Netherlands showed that sleep deprivation in children affects their attachment style. In the study, researchers measured the number of times children slept and asked their parents to complete a questionnaire that measured the child's attachment style. On average, mothers of children who slept less than eight hours per night scored higher on anxious-preoccupied attachment than mothers of children who slept longer. This indicates that sleep deprivation could be affecting the mother's ability to read the children's emotions. So, they become more anxious-preoccupied and insecure (and thus, more likely to develop an anxious-preoccupied attachment style as adults). These results were especially noticeable when the child was between 0–6 months old, as this is an important period in development when strong attachments should form in order to build trust with others.

b. Child Abuse

Child abuse can lead to an anxious-preoccupied attachment pattern as an adult because they are likely to develop hyper-vigilance and be hyper-alert to the negative behavior of others. As a result, they may become paranoid, always on the watch for betrayal, and always alert to any signs of negative behavior (which may include physical cues). This can make them feel as if they are being rejected by others which can cause anxiety and irritability.

They may also experience shame and guilt over these feelings, so they seek the help of others in order to cope with their problems (even if it is unhealthy) and develop an anxious-preoccupied attachment style as adults.

Consequently, individuals who experienced childhood abuse are more likely to develop an anxious-preoccupied attachment style.

There are two types of abuse that can lead to anxiety: verbal abuse and physical abuse. Verbal abuse involves assaults on a person's self-esteem, dignity, and reputation (e.g., calling them names, humiliating them in public, or writing nasty things about them), which may cause the person to feel confused, insecure, or a lack of confidence over how they perceive themselves. Verbal abuse may also make a person feel as if others are not hearing them and, therefore, lose trust in them.

Physical abuse involves physical force resulting in physical injury. This can cause other people to be anxious, paranoid, and hyper-alert to any physical threat (such as violence), which can make them feel as if they have to rely on others instead of themselves. This is likely because they lack self-esteem due to the fear of how others might take advantage of them (which makes them dependent).

c. Age

Children who are aged 0–5 years are expected to be very dependent on their parents, as they do not have the knowledge and skills to be independent. As a result, their attachment style tends to be anxious-preoccupied. This can cause them to become clingy for fear of being abandoned by the people who love them and can cause them to develop an anxious-preoccupied attachment (which is likely to change when they reach the age of 5).

However, it sometimes only lasts until a certain age because children have different needs between different stages in their lives. For instance, a 5-year-old child with an anxious-preoccupied attachment style may develop a more secure attachment style when they reach adolescence and start to become more independent because they can now recognize their own needs as well as the needs of others.

d. Gender

There is a link between the differences in men's and women's attachment styles. Men are more likely to develop an anxious-preoccupied attachment style as adults because they have stronger affiliation needs than women (meaning that they need to be attached to others and feel safe). Women are more likely to develop an avoidant-dismissing attachment style as adults because they have stronger intimacy needs than men, which makes them less likely to seek out others for support. This is likely to come from biology, as men are programmed to become more aggressive and assertive so that they can compete for a mate. This, in turn, makes them less dependent on others for emotional support and more accepting of rejection. On the other hand, women are programmed to be more nurturing and caring, as this is how they can compete for a mate while also raising their children effectively.

This difference may also affect how people bond with others depending on their attachment style. Women are more likely to bond with others by using an anxious-preoccupied attachment style. In contrast, men are more likely to bond with others by using a secure or avoidant-dismissing attachment style. This does not, however, imply that all women will only use an anxious-preoccupied attachment style and that all men will only use a secure or avoidant-dismissive attachment style. Instead, this likely depends on how they were brought up and socialized.

Attachment is a very important part of our lives as adults because it can affect how we perceive ourselves and others. However, the attachment style that we develop at a young age can change as we grow older and develop more complex needs. It is important to take note that you can have more than one attachment style. People who are securely attached may also develop an anxious-preoccupied attachment pattern. It all depends on the experiences of the individuals and how they cope with them.

CHAPTER 3

TRAITS OF SOMEONE WITH ANXIOUS PREOCCUPIED ATTACHMENT

The characteristic behaviors of people with an anxious preoccupied attachment include:

1. Resists Soothing or Comfort

Those with an anxious preoccupied attachment style are highly uncomfortable with being comforted in ways where they feel trapped or smothered. This is because when they were a child, the possibility of feeling safe in their environment was lost when they felt trapped by overly involved caregivers.

This trait can manifest in various ways, including:

a. Stays Away from Situations

Those anxiously preoccupied stay away from situations where they feel they are being pushed or pulled in a certain direction unless they initiate it themselves. They feel safer when they are in control of a situation and are able to leave if they want to rather than be trapped into staying due to another person's influence.

To further explain...

As a child, they may have been told to go lay down, come sit down, or get ready for bed. If the child is resistant to doing as they were told, the child will pick up on the idea that the caregiver will not listen to them or understand their actions. Due to this lack of understanding, they develop a negative belief that what they say and what they do does not matter.

This belief is further complicated by the fact that when they do try to tell others their feelings or opinions, they may be ignored or punished for it, further endowing them with the belief that their opinion or feelings do not matter, but it does not mean they have no right to have them.

b. Tend to Refuse or Reject any Form of Sympathy from Others

Due to the lack of understanding from early on and the resulting negative belief that their opinions or feelings do not matter, this child will refuse or reject any sympathy from others upon receiving it. They believe their feelings are not important or valid and will often not even consider that another person may feel bad for them.

To further explain...

Those with this type of attachment interpret the world in a way where they feel they have no right to have others feel sad for them or empathize with them. If someone was to say something like, "I'm so sorry that happened to you," they would feel uncomfortable with this display of sympathy. This is because they do not feel that how they are feeling or what happened to them is any of the person's business, so they reject the sympathy.

Before they developed this type of attachment, they may have had caregivers who told them they were a good kid, even when they were not. As those words would have been repeated again and again, they would begin to believe it in their brain. However, they would not realize that it was the caregiver's way of trying to make them feel better rather than truly believing it or believing this would be a good thing for them.

Due to this lack of understanding as a child and fear of rejection, they develop the negative perception that others are not going to like them or accept them for who they are. This belief is further complicated by their parents rejecting their feelings as well as ignoring their needs and emotions.

c. Refuses to Ask for Favors

Those with an anxious preoccupied attachment style are willing to help others or lend a hand but do not ask for favors in return. This is because they feel they need to be more worthy of others' help or that others will not be interested in what they have to offer.

To further explain...

As a child, they could have had caregivers who made them feel like their needs or feelings did not matter. They may have felt as though they were burdens to their caregivers and may have even been made to feel worthless because their needs and feelings did not matter.

This will only perpetuate the negative belief that their needs and feelings do not matter. This feeling can be further complicated by the fact that some of their caregivers may have even ignored them or punished them for having needs or feelings. This is because they felt like they were not worthy of being noticed because they did not matter and felt like their emotions were a burden to others and would only cause others to get upset with them. All combined, this could be interpreted as a child who feels that asking for help, favors, or sympathy would make others feel burdened by them; thus, they do not ask for these things.

d. Tendency to Blame Themselves for Problems

Those with an anxious preoccupied attachment style tend to blame themselves for things that are not typical for their age or situation. This is because of the negative belief that their needs and feelings do not matter and that they can do nothing about how they feel.

To further explain...

As a child, those with this type of attachment style may have been given many burdens either by their caregivers or their situation and have begun to internalize these worries. This could be anything from the family not being able to pay bills or the parent blaming them for something that was not their fault. Those who were abused physically or sexually may also internalize these worries as well as believe that what happened to them is entirely their fault despite the fact that it should never happen to anyone, regardless of how much they may be at fault for it happening.

In extreme cases, those with an anxious preoccupied attachment style may even believe that the pain they feel is their fault because some flaw in them causes it. This is because the brain believes that pain and distress are signs of weakness and that they are weak because they do not have the ability to cope with their feelings. Therefore, they internalize these feelings as a flaw in themselves rather than as a part of normal childhood development.

e. Tendency to Avoid Being Alone or Alone with Others

Those with an anxious preoccupied attachment style tend to avoid being alone or alone with other people for their own safety. For example, as a child, they could have been told that if they play alone, they will get hurt and never return. They will also have a fear of being left alone or abandoned, which can be because of the neglect they felt when growing up or the neglect shown by their caregivers.

To further explain...

As a child, those with an anxious preoccupied attachment style may have been neglected often, even if they had caregivers. Those who were neglected in this way may interpret this as an indication that their caregiver did not care about them or their needs and can further internalize the belief that their needs and feelings do not matter. This can lead to the development of a negative coping mechanism in which they prefer to be alone rather than be around others because it is safer for them. They may also believe that if they are by themselves or with others alone, no one will notice, and so it is easier for them to cope with the pain.

Even as adults, this negative coping mechanism is still present in those with an anxious preoccupied attachment style. They prefer to be alone over being observed by others because they feel alone and cut off from the rest of society. Even when there are other people around them, they will feel anxious in order not to be rejected or ignored.

2. Seems Highly Independent from an Outside Perspective

An anxious preoccupied person acts as if they are the only one in the world who matters or the only one for whom things matter, but inside, they are truly a child who feels as if their emotional experiences and needs are not being met. This is because it is easier for them to pretend they are not needy or sensitive than to risk feeling unimportant due to others not understanding their feelings.

This trait can manifest in various ways, including:

a. Tends to be Very Self-Sufficient

Anxious preoccupied people are typically very self-sufficient and tend to do things on their own. This is not because they feel they do not need help, support, or sympathy from others, but this is typically only a pretense to hide their true needs and emotions from those who would understand their experiences. They also tend to believe that if they are completely self-sufficient, others will not try to hurt or leave them.

To further explain...

As a child or an adult, those with an anxious preoccupied attachment style would have been told by their caregivers that if they were to show that they needed something or were crying, no one would want to care for them or help them. They might have been told that others did not understand their feelings and were only trying to hurt them. It would be much simpler for them to accept this than to think that someone genuinely cared about them enough to shield them from what transpired.

This fear of being cared for would eventually form a negative coping mechanism in which they would tend to be very self-sufficient. They would feel that if others were going to bother them, then they deserved it and would be more likely to feel deep resentment towards others for thinking that they could hurt or upset them. This is because this person believes any feeling of danger will always come with a threat of punishment or emotional distress from their caregivers who did not care about them after all.

b. Overly Materialistic

Anxious preoccupied people tend to believe that success and money matter to feel safe from others and their own emotional pain. This is because they feel that if they were successful, it would mean their emotional difficulties were normal and not something to be concerned about. They also feel that if they were able to have lots of money, this would show that other people do not matter as much as they may think they do.

To further explain...

As a child or an adult, those with an anxious preoccupied attachment style would have been told by their caregivers that success and material wealth did not matter in the slightest. This would only be because their caregiver was not successful and yet did not understand why such things matter. Even as a child, they would feel as if it was important to have success and wealth because, otherwise, no one would like them or care about them.

In order to cope with this feeling of rejection, they developed a negative coping mechanism in which they exaggerate the importance of material wealth. They might even become obsessed with money simply because this helps them cope with the pain and suffering caused by neglect early on in life. They feel that other people cannot help or want to be with them without money.

c. Easily Become Defensive, Argumentative, and Hastily Blame Others

Anxious preoccupied people, even when they are in a loving relationship, tend to develop an inferiority complex that can make them feel as though no one understands them or cares about their feelings. Because of this, they can become defensive at the slightest confrontation and will be more likely to blame others for things that are their own fault. As a result, it is important to show others how strong they are in order to ensure that the other person will still want to care for them and help them if needed.

To further explain...

As a child or an adult, those with an anxious preoccupied attachment style have been told by their caregivers that it was pointless to show others that they needed help or support. This is because their caregiver was always angry at them for not being able to understand their feelings or not wanting to listen to what they had to say. This is because the caregiver was upset at the fact that the child did not agree with them, cried when they did, and then wanted the parents to fix all of these problems.

In order to cope with this unpleasant experience, those with an anxious preoccupied attachment style develop an inferiority complex. Instead of trying to understand why the caregiver was so angry, they become upset at them and feel as if their anger is justified in some way. They feel as if their caregiver did not listen to or care about them, and, therefore, they have no reason to show that they need help or support. They believe it is better for them to be very defensive in order for the other person to be more likely to listen to what they have to say, just as the parents did.

d. Highly Self-Critical

Anxious preoccupied people tend to be very harsh and critical of themselves. They are very self-critical due to the fact that they believe that if something is wrong with them, then no one else will care about what happens to them. Even though this may not seem like a self-critical attitude, it is because this negative coping mechanism has prevented them from feeling comfortable or safe in the presence of other people.

To further explain...

As a child or as an adult, those with an anxious preoccupied attachment style would have been severely criticized by their caregivers, who did not understand how they felt and why they were feeling this way. They would have been told that their needs and feelings were not valid or important, which would have led them to believe that no one else could understand what they were going through or feeling. With this belief in mind, they would tend to be very harsh towards themselves because they did not see a point in feeling any better about who they are as people.

This negative coping mechanism has manifested into a very negative attitude toward other people as well. They may feel ashamed or embarrassed of who they are if others were to realize how sensitive and emotional they are. They might also fear that others will judge them in a negative way for their behavior if they were to feel too sad, angry, or upset. They are punishing themselves because they feel that they deserve to suffer as a result of how they were treated in the past.

e. Often Have a Distrust of Others

Anxious preoccupied people tend to be very distrustful of other people and tend to feel comfortable around others only when there are no expectations for things from this relationship. They will see others as potential threats to their safety and only feel comfortable around those who will not try to hurt or take advantage of them.

To further explain...

Those with an anxious preoccupied attachment style would have been raised by caregivers who were punitive and did not understand their needs. This would make it very difficult for them to trust others at all, and they would tend to be very distrustful of others regardless of the nature of the interaction. This could be because they were told that if they showed vulnerability or needed help, those around them would exploit them for their own personal gain. In order to protect themselves from this, all forms of vulnerability are avoided as much as possible, which would make it very difficult for them to feel comfortable around anyone.

This distrust of others can have a negative effect on their ability to form meaningful relationships because they feel as if no one will understand their feelings and needs. As a result, they unconsciously choose to be around people who do not demand things from them, which is often a sign of emotional neglect in adult life. They may also decide that if someone is going to hurt them or take advantage of them, then it might as well happen now because there will be no one around who can protect them or stop it from occurring.

These people are always focused on the past and feel they have to overcompensate for their mistakes to ensure that they are not judged negatively. They show this by showing others that they are someone that is independent and strong, even though they are not.

3. Not Seeming to Need Affection or Nurturance

Those with an anxious preoccupied attachment style may not seem to care about affection, nurturance, or physical contact from others. However, this is not because they do not need it but because they had been abused in these ways as a child. Anxious preoccupied types felt too trapped by their caregiver's feelings for them to feel safe expressing their own emotions.

This trait can manifest in various ways, including:

a. Unwillingness to Get Close

Anxiously preoccupied people may tend to be uncomfortable around others and have a hard time sharing what they are feeling and what they are thinking, as well as their innermost desires and thoughts. This is not because they do not want to open up to others but because they are worried about how others will react when they know the truth about who they are.

To further explain...

Anxiously preoccupied individuals want to be perceived as someone who puts others first and makes them happy at all costs. They fear being abandoned by someone they have tried so hard to please when they share who they really are with them or when they show a need for comfort or affection from the person they desire it from. They are afraid that if someone does not give them what they need, they will be left alone and eventually feel abandoned once again because they cannot stand the reality of being left alone.

Due to this, they may be very reluctant to expose themselves emotionally or physically to someone else, which makes it difficult for them to form relationships successfully over the course of their lives. They may also avoid getting close to someone for fear of being hurt again through emotional neglect, thinking, "If I can't be good enough for people, then how can I be good enough for myself?" This can lead to addictive tendencies, which are used to cope with the pain and loneliness they feel inside.

b. Tendency to Feel Disconnected

Anxious preoccupied people tend to have a very difficult time forming relationships with others because they only know how to form relationships through their thoughts, emotions, and what they do for others. There is no real feeling of connection whenever they are around other people. They will appear distant and perhaps even cold or unfriendly as a way of trying to avoid being hurt by anyone.

To further explain...

In order to feel normal or connected in any situation, anxious preoccupied types rely heavily on the feelings of others around them. These feelings allow them to feel surrounded by safety and security, thus allowing them to open up and not feel so alone inside. This is especially important if they were raised by caregivers who did not really know how to show physical affection or emotional warmth.

Anxious preoccupied people believe that no one will ever see them for who they really are when they are in circumstances where those around them only focus on what they are doing for them. Due to this, their true needs and wants never get seen and, thus, never get met, which can lead to other problems in their personal relationships, their professional relationships, and even their ability to form new relationships.

c. Impatience

Anxious preoccupied types tend to be impatient in relationships because they are afraid to give a little and try new things out. They feel as though they have to talk about a lot of different things at once but only have enough time to tell the truth about what they are thinking, what their true emotions are, and what their wants and needs are. It is very difficult for them to be patient with someone else when all of these feelings get mixed up and confused in their own head.

To further explain...

Anxiously preoccupied types fear having meaningful relationships because it is too much effort for them to get close to someone else. To them, it would take too much energy and too much time to really show someone else who they are. For example, they would not be able to tell anyone their true feelings and needs without feeling extremely vulnerable and fearful of being hurt. They tend to stay guarded around others with whom they are trying to develop a relationship out of the fear that others will not understand them or will think them crazy for how they feel about the people in their lives.

Being around other people makes them feel as if they are being judged and being put on trial for things they have not done in their life thus far. They feel as though others do not really want to listen to them and instead want to get what they can for themselves out of the situation. Because of this, they may feel the need to speak over the other person, making it difficult for the other person to get a word in.

d. Being Overly Accommodating

Anxious preoccupied types tend to be very accommodating in relationships because they are scared that someone else in their life might decide to abandon them or not give them what they need. Again, this is not because they seek to make others happy, but rather because when someone makes them happy, they feel loved and desired for who they truly are.

To further explain...

Prioritizing others helps anxiously preoccupied individuals feel as though they are a part of something greater than themselves. They strive to achieve the feeling of being loved for who they are by doing whatever it takes to be valued and appreciated by others. In this process, however, they may end up going out of their way to make others happy without ever really thinking about how it may affect them or how much it really costs them.

Being overly accommodating can lead to many problems in a person's life, especially when those people to whom they are overly accommodating do not appreciate their efforts and take advantage of this. Some anxious preoccupied types may also be so taken up with showing their great care and concern for others that they become too attached to them at the expense of actually caring about what is going on in their own lives. This can make it very difficult for them to form relationships with people they do not know or have had no real prior relationships with.

e. Inability to Identify and Express Feelings

Those with an anxious preoccupied adult attachment style may have a difficult time identifying and expressing their feelings, ideas, and thoughts until it is too late. For example, they may continue to hold on to the anger they feel over others' mistakes in past relationships while seeing the person who harmed them as someone who will never hurt them again.

They tend to keep their fears and thoughts bottled up inside them, which can result in short tempers or sudden mood swings that might seem to come out of nowhere to others. It is important to note, however, that this is not necessarily because they are in a bad mood or did it on purpose to upset or anger someone else.

To further explain...

Anxiously preoccupied people have difficulty identifying and expressing anger because they have not been given the outlet to express themselves freely. As a result, they may still hold on to these feelings when they find an outlet in other relationships to release them. This is not to say that they are consciously doing this, but by expressing their anger out of turn, it might be their way of trying to gain control over their inability to express anger in the past.

Anxiously preoccupied people find it difficult to express their anger because they lack a healthy way to vent this. They may feel as though getting angry is wrong because it demonstrates that they need nurturance and support to cope with the pain of being with someone, which their caregiver did not provide for them. It is unlikely that someone will be able to deal with others' anger if they do not know how to do so in a healthy way.

This behavior of not seeming to need affection and especially not seeming to need love or care leads to adults complaining about feeling lonely and unloved when they have a great deal of love and care for others but are unable to express it.

4. Considerably More Anxious Than They Project

Anxious preoccupied people tend to be considerably more anxious than they project, and they can be less self-assured and more anxious than they seem on the outside. They do not do things to look anxious or appear unsure of themselves, but they have a lot of anxiety on the inside that is not apparent in their actions.

This trait can manifest in various ways, including:

a. Quick to Get Riled Up

Anxious preoccupied people usually get riled up by the slightest thing, which might make someone else uncomfortable around them, even if they themselves did not do anything wrong. This can make it difficult for other people to sit down and talk with them, especially since they are so quick to get angry and upset at the smallest of inanities.

To further explain...

Those with anxious preoccupied attachment styles are raised by caregivers who are critical and disparaging towards them. This would make it very difficult for them to feel good in peoples' presences or feel as if others are interested in what they have to say. In order to protect themselves from this, they subconsciously overcompensate for their negative feelings towards others by becoming quick to become upset or angry at any given moment. This trait makes it much easier for them to appear threatening around others because they have developed a very tough exterior that no one can seem to crack.

Because they appear to be so easily angered, this behavior can make it impossible to have a conversation with the individual. It is also common for them to appear uninterested in conversing with anyone, despite the fact that this may not be the case. Their lack of trust in other people makes it very difficult to open up and talk about what is really bothering them and why they feel as if they are having these feelings.

b. Overly Concerned About Others

Anxiously preoccupied people tend to be overly concerned about other people. They may worry a lot about how others feel or what they are thinking and are often willing to do whatever is necessary to ensure that their relationships remain in good order. However, because they are so worried about others and how those others might feel about them, they often fail to consider needs of their own. Instead, anxiously preoccupied types might be too busy worrying about whether the other person is happy with them rather than asking themselves whether they are truly happy with themselves.

To further explain...

Although anxiously preoccupied types are generally more concerned about other people than themselves, this does not mean they do not worry about how others might view them. For example, they may try to put on a happy face when they are with others, even when they feel extremely unhappy with themselves, to make others feel better. In fact, these people can make anyone around them feel good even though underneath it all, the anxiety eating at them is truly making them unhappy.

They do so in order to serve as an emotional pillar for others. Because they have experienced pain themselves, they are prepared to do anything to spare others from suffering the same fate. At the same time, however, they do not want to let others know that they are hurting because they want to make others happy. They are aware that other people are not feeling good, so they make the conscious choice to put on a happy face to make sure that others feel better about themselves.

c. Sometimes Overly Serious About Things That Are Not Threatening

Anxiously preoccupied people tend to become very serious and earnest when dealing with various situations in their lives, which often makes them seem threatening to other people. This is because the anxiety eating at them is not making them smile or laugh, so smiling and laughing would not be natural for them.

To further explain...

Anxiously preoccupied people are very serious about things that do not seem to require too much emotional effort on their part. For example, when someone has a negative feeling about something and does not know what to do with it, anxiously preoccupied types may go through the same motions that they took when they were children with their parents. They also will take on a serious demeanor as if they understand everything that is going on around them, even though this may be a pretense. This is because they are not yet ready to be seen as happy and carefree, so they must maintain their appearance of being emotionally stable and instantly capable of handling any situation that might arise.

This can make it seem as if they are threatening or angry with others because they do not appear as if they are actively enjoying themselves. In fact, other people might even take them to be seriously unhappy, which is very far from the truth.

d. Can Be Unpredictable

Anxiously preoccupied people can be very unpredictable in their emotions and reactions toward others. Although this does not mean that all of their responses are negative, it does imply that a lot of emotional energy goes into the positive ones, making them somewhat difficult to deal with and understand at times.

To further explain...

Anxiously preoccupied people tend to have a unique and complicated way of thinking about emotions that differ from most other people. When they are feeling good, they tend to be really happy and carefree. However, if they do not feel good, they will often react in ways that are quite serious and intense. These kinds of responses can make them appear threatening because those around them will not know how to respond when their moods change so quickly and with no warning. For example, their smiles may seem forced and unnatural in public settings. They may become angry or upset for no apparent reason, even though there is nothing on the horizon to cause such a response. Furthermore, they may begin to cry for reasons that remain unexplained and which they themselves may not even be aware of.

Additionally, their unpredictability may make it difficult for them to understand their own emotions from moment to moment. They might go from being sad and feeling sorry for themselves to being very happy for no apparent reason at all. This sudden change in mood and emotion can make them feel very confused about what is actually making them feel the way that they do, which will only add to their problem because it will make it harder for them to understand what is really going on inside of them.

e. Worried About Others Regardless of When or Where

Most anxiously preoccupied people are overprotective and constantly worry about how others view them, even when they are somewhere where they can see that someone else is not going to be able to cause them any harm. This makes it very hard for them to relax because they are always afraid that someone might be able to do something to hurt them. This behavior is especially true for those who have suffered childhood abuse or neglect.

To further explain...

In general, preoccupied people tend to focus on what is happening around them. Those with an anxious attachment will typically differ from these other types of people in that they also focus on what may happen around others at some point in the future.

Anxiously preoccupied people are more likely to worry about how other people might hurt them in some way or another in the future. They usually try to prevent this imagined outcome by instead putting the focus on trying to protect others over themselves.

Anxiously preoccupied people usually have a lot on their minds. They are always thinking about what might happen to them if they were to let their guard down, and it is often very difficult for them to get a clear head because of this. They will be harsh and impatient with others, even when those others might not deserve it. Anxious preoccupied individuals can become paranoid over the smallest of things because their thoughts are constantly on the subject of how someone else might do something bad to them or leave them just when they need that person the most.

This trait makes it very difficult for the anxiously preoccupied to display many of the positive traits of being healthy and happy. This is because they are making it their goal to be perceived as a "good" person while actually living out their lives in a very unhealthy and unbalanced way.

5. Seeks Proximity but Avoids Contact

The anxious preoccupied type may attempt to seek proximity with others but still avoid physical contact.

This can be displayed in their behaviors in a number of ways, including:

a. Wanting to Be Close but Not Close Enough

People with this type of attachment style may be able to spend time with others without physical contact. They may feel they want to get close to others but will not risk asking for physical affection or care from the people they desire this from. Their relationship history has shown them that it is much safer if other people do not see how much they need and desire affection. Therefore, they do not ask for it and keep their feelings toward others to themselves so that no one realizes just how needy and dependent upon others for support and love they actually are.

To further explain...

People with anxious preoccupied attachment styles have been raised in households where their caregivers may not have allowed them to, or did not allow them to, get too close to others. This makes it difficult for them to share their feelings and thoughts with others and also makes it hard for them to open themselves up physically. They frequently grow up in families with little emotional support because their parents may not have had much support when they were kids themselves. This can leave the child feeling as if they should be able to do this while simultaneously causing tremendous amounts of anxiety within the child because they do not feel as though they will ever be able to make it without the support of others.

This type of anxiety can cause them to feel great amounts of discomfort when they are around others, especially if they have been rejected in the past or had a need for warmth or comfort that their caregivers did not meet. It can also make them feel as if they cannot express themselves to others and need emotional support because of the fear that their feelings toward someone else will not be reciprocated, which causes them to have feelings of abandonment in their lives. This can leave them feeling alone amidst the crowd, which they have experienced before, and they choose to avoid these feelings again.

b. Violating Their Boundaries

Many anxious preoccupied people will have a hard time defining their boundaries with others so that they are not intruding on the personal space of others. As a result, they may find it challenging to decide whether to touch others because they will generally try to avoid all contact, especially physical contact.

To further explain...

Anxiously preoccupied types are typically raised in households where physical boundaries were not properly defined for them. This causes them to feel as though they should have been physically able to touch others without fear of being abused by those people. They will constantly be thinking about violating the boundaries of others and doing so whenever possible because their parents never taught them that it is wrong to do this when the other person does not want to be touched by them.

When they become adults, anxiously preoccupied people often continue violating the boundaries of others simply because they do not feel as if it is ever going to be more socially acceptable for them to do so. This leads them down a road of being judgmental and critical of others because they feel that is all they have known in their lives thus far, which gives them a hard time when trying to decide if other people are doing the same thing to them, or maybe they do not know any better yet. It is very rare for this type of person to be able to set proper boundaries for themselves because their caregivers were not able to teach them how to do so.

c. Feel Like One Foot In, One Foot Out

Many anxious preoccupied types will feel as though they want to be close to other people but do not want to be that close actually. They will feel as though they are already emotionally entangled with others in some way, and so it would be a lot safer for them if they were to maintain physical distance between themselves and their relationship partners. This can cause them to feel like they always have one foot out of their relationships and often leaves them confused about why they really want more from the relationship, even though they are trying to avoid it simultaneously. They will often fear having to really open up from the start because it is something that they have never done before and cannot see a way through doing so without it causing them to feel too overwhelmed, which is something that is a given for people with this attachment style.

To further explain...

Anxiously preoccupied people have been raised by caregivers who did not teach them proper boundaries. This causes them to feel as though they feel "too close" to others, and it does not make sense for them at all when trying to figure out why they are doing what they are doing. They want to be in their relationship but do not want to get too close without realizing that they are already too close, even though they do not understand how this happened.

They constantly feel as if they are about to lose control of themselves when around their partners and often feel as though they need to hide a part of themselves from them so that others will not see just how anxious and insecure they truly feel inside on the most basic level. It is very common for anxiously preoccupied people to stay in relationships with partners who treat them poorly because it is all they know, making it a lot easier for them to stay in those relationships than to try and leave them behind. When they leave these types of relationships, they often feel as though they are leaving a part of themselves behind and cannot seem to move on from that relationship, even though it causes them a great deal of anxiety to think about the past.

d. Need to Get "Into the Flow."

Anxiously preoccupied people often need to find a balance between being able to feel as though they are able to get into a flow state and then being able to pull out of it at any second without being in danger of feeling as if they are losing themselves. They will engage in very complex behaviors that can be difficult for them to explain otherwise because their feelings of anxiety often cause them to engage in odd behavior that others would not see.

To further explain...

Anxiously preoccupied people need to feel as though they are reaching a balance between the world around them and their inner selves. They will often engage in a repetitive activity, like taking a shower, until they feel as though their body is relaxed enough to be able to feel like they can open up emotionally and let themselves become vulnerable with the people who are closest to them. This causes them to have a hard time explaining why they do what they do because it all comes down to this balance that they must reach to experience emotional intimacy with others. The more anxious they become, the more vulnerable they feel, and the harder it will be for them to find their balance before any of those feelings overrun their entire being.

e. Shying Away from Physical Contact

People with anxious preoccupied attachment styles will often try to avoid physical contact with others because they are afraid they may need this type of attention from them and will not receive it. They do not want to get too close to others because they worry that it is too much comfort and attention that they cannot give back to the other person because they have had very little of this type of care in their lives. It is possible for them to believe that if someone has held them as a child, then the person will only use this as a means to care for them again and use their next interaction with this individual as a means to gain more attention for themselves.

To further explain...

It is common for anxiously preoccupied people to be brought up in households that are not able to provide much affection or care for them. This can leave them feeling as if they are not capable of giving this care to others, which makes it even more difficult for them to do so without having some sort of negative effect. They may believe that if someone has allowed them to touch or hold them in the past, they can use it to get their attention in the future because they want more of what they have been given in the past.

It is also possible for these individuals to be afraid of what other people will think of them if they allow themselves to get too close, which can cause them to avoid getting close for the discomfort of being seen and possibly judged by others. Most people see this as shyness because it is difficult for them to understand why they are so hesitant to get close in the first place when they have had ample comfort and affection from others before.

The need to seek proximity but avoid contact is predicated on a fear of rejection or abandonment from not being accepted by those who may offer comfort or affection. The anxiety blocking the integration of memories and feelings causes this ambivalence.

Attachment, developed in early childhood and maintained through adulthood, is fundamental to one's experience of security and self-worth. The anxious preoccupied style is characterized by an extreme desire for attachment and an intense fear of rejection that can make it difficult for the individual to achieve a positive sense of self.

PART 2

WHAT EFFECT DOES ANXIOUS PREOCCUPIED ATTACHMENT HAVE ON RELATIONSHIPS?

CHAPTER 4

THE EFFECTS OF ANXIOUS PREOCCUPIED ATTACHMENT ON ROMANTIC RELATIONSHIP

Your attachment style directly affects your relationships. Attachment styles are a good indicator of how a person handles emotional intimacy; therefore, individuals with different styles behave differently in relationships.

HOW ANXIOUS PREOCCUPIED PRESENT THEMSELVES ROMANTICALLY

The following is how someone with an anxious preoccupied attachment style presents themselves romantically:

1. Overdependency

Those with this attachment style tend to be overly dependent on their partners for both emotional and physical support.

What can trigger this trait?

The following things can trigger this trait:

a. Feeling insecure

Anxious-preoccupied individuals tend to feel unsure about their partner's feelings or intentions and, therefore, will feel insecure and require excessive attention. This is because if they are always thinking about their partner, they will feel reassured that the partner is still interested and cares for them. This behavior is from a desire to create a sense of security surrounding their relationship.

For example...

You may find yourself needing regular reassurance that your partner still loves or cares for you. You tend to ask your partner a lot of questions about their feelings for you, especially when you are insecure about something. You do things to try and make them feel obligated to you and show them that you are still there for them. Even though your partner might have told you they love you or still care for you, it does not make you feel any less insecure. This is because no matter what your partner tells you, it can be difficult to take their word for it, which is why you continue to ask for reassurance that they still care.

While this may seem like a good tactic to ensure that your partner does care for you and will be there for you, this may lead to your partner becoming annoyed with you. This insecurity will make you feel dependent on your partner for support and comfort. They might feel you are being too needy and not giving them enough space. This can make them feel obligated to give you what you ask for, aggravating them even more.

Remember that constantly asking for reassurance will only make your partner feel as though they need to give you answers that make you happy, which may eventually lead to them resenting you because of all the questions you keep asking them.

b. Feeling isolated

Anxious preoccupied individuals tend to feel very isolated in their relationships. They will often feel an emotional need to constantly be physical with their partner, especially if they feel they don't have anyone else to talk to. This is because an anxious preoccupied individual needs a constant partner who will make them feel safe and secure and can help them avoid triggers that might cause them to feel anxious.

For example...

You feel as though you are constantly in need of your partner's company. You feel like you cannot go anywhere or do anything without your lover at your side. Because of this, you may feel as though your partner is your only source of comfort. You experience severe anxiety at the thought of being apart from your partner or not having them by your side all the time, so you will go to great lengths to keep them there. You might do this by being clingy or just wanting to be in the same space as them. This can make your partner feel as though they have to constantly keep up with you and keep you happy, or else you would become desperate for attention or something.

While it is important to have an emotional support system, remember that being too clingy towards your partner may result in them feeling trapped or even suffocated, especially if they are someone who feels as though they are quite independent. If your partner constantly feels as though they have to keep up with you and ensure you are always happy and secure, it will only lead to resentment on their part. This is why you should not think of having a constant physical companion but a supportive and loving partner who will care for you and ensure you are always happy, but not so much that it suffocates.

Remember that having a partner whom you depend on too much will only lead to them not wanting to be around you or have contact with you. And if they do eventually feel as though they have had enough of your clinginess, they are free to leave or distance themselves from you.

c. Feeling insecure

Anxious-preoccupied individuals tend to feel unsure about their partner's feelings or intentions and, therefore, will feel insecure and require excessive attention. This is because if they are always thinking about their partner, they will feel reassured that the partner is still interested and cares for them. This behavior is from a desire to create a sense of security surrounding their relationship.

For example...

You may find yourself needing constant reassurance that your partner still loves and cares for you. You tend to ask your partner a lot of questions about their feelings for you, especially when you are insecure about something. You do things to try and make them feel obligated to you and to show them that you are still there for them. Even though your partner might have told you they love you or still care for you, it does not make you feel any less insecure. This is because no matter what your partner tells you, it can be difficult to take their word for it, which is why you continue to ask for reassurance that they still care.

While this may seem like a good tactic to ensure your partner cares for you and will be there for you, this may lead to your partner becoming annoyed with you. This insecurity will make you dependent on your partner for support and comfort. They might feel you are being too needy and not giving them enough space. This can make them feel obligated to give you what you ask for, aggravating them even more.

Remember that constantly asking for reassurance will only make your partner feel as though they need to give you answers that make you happy, which may eventually lead to them resenting you because of all the questions you keep asking them.

d. Intrusive Thoughts

Anxious-preoccupied individuals are more prone to having intrusive thoughts than people without this attachment style. These thoughts are not just about themselves but also about their partner. Because of this, intrusive thoughts will cause them to have difficulty concentrating, as they will have to think about these disturbing thoughts, and the only escape from them is through depending on their partner. They will do anything to avoid these thoughts, which will result in a need to have their partner present or with them. They will feel as though their partner has the power to keep them from these thoughts.

For example...

When you have intrusive thoughts, whether about your partner or not, you may feel as if your partner's presence is enough to prevent these thoughts from entering your mind. Even though this might be true, it does not help in overcoming these intrusive thoughts. You will not be able to think about anything else but these thoughts, and this is why you will need your partner with you or nearby. You might even want them to stay with you all the time. It is as if the only way for you to be at peace is for your partner to always be there because it might help prevent these thoughts from coming.

Remember that having excessive and constant thoughts in your mind can be debilitating and consuming. They can cause major distress and anxiety and eventually take away the motivation to do things or enjoy social activities. It may make it seem as if there is no escape from them and that your partner is the only way to make you feel better.

The overdependence that people with an anxious preoccupied attachment style have on others can be a form of behavior to ease the anxieties and uncertainty they feel about their own emotions as well as a way to take care of the relationship. Because they are so dependent on their partners, they are often willing to do anything and everything to feel secure and safe, even if it is unfair in the long term.

2. High Jealousy Levels

Anxiously preoccupied people tend to have high jealousy levels due to their partner's attention shifting from themselves to others. They are highly sensitive and will thus feel jealous in most situations, which may cause a change in attention between themselves and their partner.

What can trigger this trait?

This can be triggered by:

a. Mentioning Past Relationships

If their partner has mentioned their past relationships, those with an anxious preoccupied attachment will tend to have a high jealousy level. This is because they believe that if their partner has had a past relationship, it means that they are more inclined to leave them and will choose someone else.

For example...

You might find yourself feeling jealous of your partner if they mention their past relationships. Even if you know they have always been faithful to you, the thought of your partner having other experiences will make you feel insecure about your relationship with them. You will then constantly be worried that if a better option comes along, your partner will choose to be with them instead of you. So, you will try to keep them occupied with you and as far as possible from anyone that might cause a shift in attention.

Your excessive jealousy will make you feel possessive of your partner, and it will be difficult for you to share them with others unless it is convenient for you. Even though they may not be doing anything wrong, their past relationships will constantly cause you to worry about your relationship with them.

Remember that just because your partner has had previous relationships does not mean they are more likely to commit adultery or to leave their current partner for someone else. You never know what the future might bring or what people are capable of doing; remember that everyone deserves a second chance.

b. Annoying Behavior

Anxious preoccupied individuals may feel jealous due to their partner's annoying behavior. If their partner seems to be always complaining about something, being irritable, or going on about things that are not even true, these people will tend to feel a high level of jealousy. This is because they believe that if their partner is going on about something, it means that they will end up leaving them for someone else. They then believe that if they attempt to stop their partner from doing this, they will be ignored, and the relationship will deteriorate.

For example...

You may have felt jealous when your partner was constantly complaining about everything. You may have then tried to ignore them, but this did not help. You ended up feeling as if your partner was not happy with you anymore and that they might leave you for someone who does not complain as much. This will cause you to feel possessive of your partner and try to prevent them from doing anything that may jeopardize their relationship with you.

Likewise, if your partner constantly complains about everything, is in a bad mood, and something else could be bothering them, it is important that you check on them and see what is wrong in order to avoid any trouble that may be caused. Do not allow them to take this bad mood out on you, and don't treat them as if they are being unreasonable. You must be there for them and allow them the opportunity to express their emotions to you.

Remember that just because your partner is complaining about something does not mean they are unhappy with the relationship. It could be a temporary problem, and complaining might be their way of expressing themselves. Don't immediately jump to conclusions, and try to talk to your partner about what is wrong so that you can avoid any unnecessary trouble in the long run.

c. Changes in their Behavior

Changes in your partner's behavior may cause you to become jealous. This is because you will be more aware of your partner's actions and activities, and those with anxious preoccupied attachment place a lot of expectations on them. You will hold them to a high standard, and it will be challenging for them to live up to your expectations.

For example...

The presence of a new person around your partner may cause you to think about all the other new people that are in your partner's life, so the thought that they are getting too much attention becomes an issue for you. You would rather your partner not have these new people around and only be with you, but they will appear again, making you more irritated by their behavior.

Your excessive expectations will make you feel as if there is no way that your partner could live up to them. This will cause you to feel possessive of your partner and try to prevent them from doing anything that may jeopardize their relationship with you. They may not do anything wrong or even intend to, but you will still become jealous.

Remember that it is normal for a partner to have relationships with other people outside of your relationship. Your partner may be friends with others, but they will still be your partner, and they are not allowed to break the relationship between you two.

d. Your Partner's Appearance

Anxious preoccupied individuals may also become jealous because they believe that if their partner looks attractive, they will be more likely to leave them. This is because they believe that if their partner has an attractive appearance, it means that other people will want to be with them. Anxious people will see this as a sign of a better relationship and will begin thinking about leaving their love for someone more attractive. Then, they become envious of this attractive person, whom you perceive to be superior to yourself.

For example...

Your partner's appearance might not have anything to do with your jealousy, but it could make you feel jealous of another individual in their life whom they seem to want the most attention from. You will start thinking about their previous relationships where they have been with other people that are more attractive than you. You don't think anyone would leave you for them, but you do not want to risk losing your partner for someone else.

In order to avoid your partner's unrealistic expectations, you need to give them space from their friends. Your partner is always free to socialize with friends, but it is important that you are there for them in case they want to leave once again. If this does happen, then you should be ready for the possibility of a breakdown in the relationship.

Remember that just because your partner has a lot of friends, it does not mean that they are breaking the relationship between you two. They will always be your partner and always be there for you. You need to give them their space in order to see if their feelings for you are still the same.

The high level of jealousy in someone with this attachment style will cause them to feel irritated by their partner. They will then begin to act on their feelings of jealousy, thinking that they are protecting their relationship. This behavior can eventually lead to problems within the relationship itself and can be associated with other mental health disorders, such as depression.

They may feel they are being treated unfairly because they believe their partner is always putting them down in various ways.

3. Unstable Communication

Anxiously preoccupied people will experience sudden shifts in communication between themselves and their partners. They will act distant or not communicate at all and then suddenly become very talkative, sometimes even obsessive. This happens because their feelings can be very intense, and they don't want to hurt their partner. But this usually ends with the partner feeling ignored, even if they have not been ignoring their partner, and they end up feeling like something is wrong.

What can trigger this trait?

a. Changes due to External Events

These people will experience sudden shifts in their behavior because of things that may happen that they do not expect, like unexpected visitors or phone calls, or even something small, like an article of clothing being misplaced. These changes can cause great discomfort or even anger, which will result in the anxious preoccupied person not talking to their partner or acting distant out of anger. This will usually lead to their partner questioning them and feeling confused by their sudden change in behavior.

For example...

You tend to get upset when unexpected and unimportant things happen, like today's newspaper article about your partner being political, or you lost a toothbrush this morning. These trivial matters have nothing to do with your relationship, but they will irritate and anger you, causing you to become estranged from your partner.

Your partner will be confused about how you change your behavior and begin feeling like something is wrong in the relationship. When they try to talk to you about it, you will brush them off and tell them it is nothing important. Then, things will become more distant, and you won't be very open with one another, which makes your partner feel confused and upset. They will begin to believe that something is wrong with them or that their partner has lost interest in their life.

There is nothing wrong with getting upset when things like this happen, but it is important that you do not let your emotions and feelings control the relationship. It's crucial to communicate your feelings to your partner, be open and honest with them, and control your emotions as much as possible.

Remember that if you are feeling upset, it is okay to explain to your partner that you are upset about something, but do not let this start an argument about the event that upset you. Try to be honest and open, and try to avoid acting distant or withdrawn from your partner.

b. Short-Term Goals not Achieved

An anxious-preoccupied person will make many plans for their future and for their relationship with their partner, but when these plans do not pan out the way they want them to, this will cause them to become very upset, which will result in them starting to avoid their partner or withdrawing from them. Then, they will feel as though they have failed in their relationship and future planning because their partner's goals, like a holiday or family vacation, won't be achieved.

For example...

You are dissatisfied with your current position, but you believe you will soon be happier because your supervisor has promised you a promotion within two months. Your partner asks if they can go on a trip as soon as possible so that you can spend more time together, and you refuse, saying that it will not be possible until you are promoted. This makes your partner feel upset, and they begin withdrawing from you, which in turn makes you feel hurt and annoyed.

Your partner will feel disappointed in you because they know how much they have given up to get where they are. They will begin feeling angry at you and blaming themself. This can be very painful for both of you because you have spent a lot of time planning this trip, but it has not happened yet. So, you will both feel very hurt, which can cause you to be distant.

Keep in mind that it is acceptable not to want to do something, but you should still be honest with your partner. If you are honest with them, they will respect you for it and understand your feelings without needing to blame themself or withdraw from you. It is important that you understand their feelings, too, so that when they have feelings about something happening in the future, that could turn out like this example has. You will then know what to tell them to make them feel comfortable again.

c. Uncertainty and Anxiety

These people will experience sudden changes in their behavior because of uncertainty and anxiety about their own actions. They will often feel that they need to be living up to their partner's expectations or are doing something wrong with the relationship by either not spending enough or too much time together. This uncertainty, again, makes them feel as if their partner is always judging them and looking down on them.

For example...

You've been married for a year, but during that time, you've never gone to hang out with your friends. You only see them on the weekends with your partner, and you feel as though they are beginning to think that you do not enjoy their company anymore or that you do not want to spend time with them because they always suggest going out together. Every time they suggest this, you make an excuse to avoid it. Your partner has begun withdrawing from you, which makes you extremely upset with yourself because you know that your friends are important to you, and even if they are not right now, they will be again when the time is right.

Your partner will feel as though you are never spending enough time with them or that they are not attractive to you anymore. It would help if you made them understand that your friends are still important to you and that you would like to spend time with them, too. It is important that you do this without making excuses or crying about it. Just let them know what is happening and talk about why it makes sense for both of you to spend time together instead of living in a world where one person thinks their partner does not want them around anymore because their behavior has changed in some way.

d. Relationship Stress

Anxious preoccupied individuals frequently believe they are falling short of their partner's expectations and are perpetually failing in their relationship. This can cause them to become very self-conscious and insecure in their relationship, which makes them want to withdraw. It makes them feel as if everything is always turning against them or that something bad will happen. They genuinely believe something will go wrong in the relationship or that something could happen at any time, so it's not just them thinking these things.

For example...

Your partner has had a difficult day at work, and when you ask them what happened, they say they cannot tell you because they do not want to upset you. This makes you feel as though they are concealing something. This can be anything from a big deal at work to a small problem with a co-worker that upsets them. If they cannot share these things with you, how do you know there is no other secret about them that makes them act this way? You begin to feel angry and withdraw from your partner, which in turn makes them feel hurt and confused, thinking that because they have not told you what happened today, it must mean that there is something very wrong with the relationship.

Your partner will feel as though they are trying so hard to make you happy, but nothing is working, making them feel like they are a failure in the relationship. They begin to worry about it and believe that there is something wrong with their marriage and that everything is not going well. This behavior can be very hurtful for both of you, and because your partner feels this way, they will begin withdrawing from you even though the issue may have been minor, or it may have been just something on their mind. It would help if you talked with them about what happened and why they did not want you to know about it to understand why they acted the way they did.

The unstable communication you show damages your relationship and overall well-being. It causes you to feel insecure in the relationship, and if it persists for too long, it may lead to you or your partner withdrawing from each other. This will make the problem worse because you both now want to avoid each other, which causes everything that comes with it. To resolve these issues and strengthen your relationship, you and your partner must learn how to communicate effectively with one another. Once you do this, then all of the behavior that comes with it will stop and leave behind strong communication and love for one another because of it.

4. Shallow Emotional Depth

Those with an anxious preoccupied attachment style often display shallow emotional depth. They are prone to emotional outbursts, which may make it difficult for them to share emotional information or feelings that they may have about issues within relationships. This can result in a tendency to avoid discussing their feelings, which may make them appear aloof and uncaring to their partner.

What can trigger this trait?

a. Counteracting Differential Treatment.

This style is most likely to respond to a wide variety of situations, which may cause them to react abruptly or not respond in a timely manner. They may appear as though they are not listening or do not care about what the other person has said, especially if the other person is being critical of them. They may become very angry in response, which can make it difficult for them to respond calmly and effectively when it is time for them to speak up.

For example...

You believe your partner is treating you unfairly, but you do not want to express this because it would make it more difficult for them to respect you and your feelings. You believe that if you express how they make you feel, they will not like you and may view you as a bad person or believe you have a defect. You decide to withdraw from your partner instead because it will hurt less to keep this inside and say nothing rather than have them ask you to tell them how they make you feel, which makes you not want to tell them. You will then be unable to communicate effectively when it comes time for you to speak up about something that is bothering you.

This may cause your partner to feel hurt and confused because they do not understand why you are acting the way that you are. This is for the same reason that you are unable to tell them how they make you feel when asked. They will begin to think that there is something wrong with the relationship or that there is something wrong with them because they cannot seem to get through to you. They then begin to withdraw from you and shut down because they feel something is wrong with them, making you feel like you are the problem. These feelings then cause your partner to step back from your relationship and make it harder for them to listen when it comes time for you to speak up.

These situations will continue to happen between the two of you until you learn how to communicate effectively. Once this happens, you will be able to discuss your feelings with each other and work through these issues, which will make it easier for the two of you to communicate on a regular basis.

b. Attributions of Insecurity.

Those in this style are often very insecure about their relationship, making it difficult for them to open up to those around them and share how they feel with others. They do not like being vulnerable and may feel that their partner will judge them based on their feelings, making it difficult for them to tell their partner how they feel about things when asked. This can prevent them from discussing relationship-related issues that need to be addressed or that may be bothering them.

For example...

You are afraid of your partner judging you based on your feelings and do not want to look weak or scared in front of them. You do not want to seem weak or unsure of yourself, and this causes you to show little or no emotion when your partner tries to get you to open up or speak about things that are bothering you.

This makes it difficult for them to know what is wrong with you, making them feel they cannot help you. They begin to withdraw from the relationship and close down because they do not know how to help if they cannot identify their partner's issue. They cannot try and help to make it easier for you to speak up about your feelings and open up about things that are bothering you. These feelings will leave behind a difficult relationship for the two of you to communicate in, which will cause more issues between the two of you and make it harder to discuss important issues that need to be addressed within the relationship.

c. Denial of Emotional Pain.

Those with an anxious preoccupied attachment style are often unable to recognize when their partner is experiencing emotional pain or distress within a close relationship due to their own inability to express or share their own emotions, as well as their partner's inability or unwillingness to share theirs. This can cause them to overlook their partner's needs or problems and may make them feel as if they are not there for each other or are not in a strong relationship.

For example...

You and your partner begin to fight because you do not want to talk about something that is bothering you. Your partner then tells you that it is no big deal, which makes you angry and upset because you are frustrated that they do not understand how upset this makes you feel. You then take all of your anger out on them and become very defensive about it, which causes your partner to become very defensive themself so they can get their point across about how little this means to them. The two of you then begin to argue and cannot tell each other that you are hurt or upset because you feel they do not care or are just not listening.

The two of you then withdraw from each other and become very defensive when it comes time to speak up about something that is bothering both of you. You may feel like you need clarification as to where the conflict began, which can make it difficult for you to speak up about things that are bothering you. This can cause a cycle in your relationship, in which neither one of you can say anything to the other that will make them understand how upset or hurt they have made them feel.

d. Mistrust-Based Responses.

Those with an anxious preoccupied attachment style tend to be very distrusting of their partner and may feel as if they cannot trust them to keep their emotions under control. This can make them feel as if they cannot trust their partner not to lose their temper when something is bothering them or that they cannot trust that their partner will not shut down and become withdrawn when faced with a problem within the relationship.

For example...

You and your partner are discussing something that is bothering you, and your partner begins to get frustrated because they disagree with how you are handling the situation. They then get frustrated with you and begin to yell at you, which makes you feel as if they do not care about what is bothering you and are only being mean because they see something in your behavior that bothers them. You then take all of your anger out on them and feel as if they do not understand the situation and do not listen to what is bothering you. You may ask them how they could be so mean without listening to what is bothering you, which causes your partner to become very defensive in order to try and correct their behavior.

The two of you begin to withdraw from each other when it comes time for you to discuss things that are bothering or upsetting you within the relationship. The behavior of the two of you will leave you feeling as if the other does not care about what is bothering or upsetting you, which can cause confusion and either make it difficult for you to talk about things that are bothering you or make it difficult for your partner to talk to you about what is bothering them.

The shallow emotional depth in someone with this attachment style leads them to see their partner as only being there to serve their own needs and not there to support them and help them in their personal relationships.

5. Lack of Commitment

Anxiously preoccupied individuals do not commit to romantic relationships and will only be loyal during the early stages of a relationship. They will begin to feel trapped by their partner if the relationship gets too serious and they do not see any exit options. This is because they cannot see their partner as anything more than a confidant or source of emotional support, making them more likely to break off a serious relationship when they cannot get the support they want from their partner. They would rather leave first than have their partner leave them.

What can trigger this trait?

a. Partner's Instability.

Every time the partner of those with this type of attachment style shows signs that they may become unstable, they begin to see them as a threat. Instability means they do not value the relationship like they should and may leave it at any moment. This can cause them to distance themself from their partner and begin thinking that the relationship is not as strong or good as it once was, making it easier for them to end the relationship and search for another partner they feel is more stable.

For example...

You begin a relationship with someone, and they are very loving and caring towards you, which makes you very happy. You are then surprised when they start to pull away from you to spend time with their friends or family members, making you feel as if the relationship is no longer as strong as it once was. You begin to feel as if your partner has lost interest in the relationship and are confused about how this has happened. You become unsure about your role in the relationship and begin to feel as if you are no longer important to them.

The thought of your partner leaving you for someone else will intensify and make you feel like you are no longer good enough for them. You start to feel like you're being left behind, so you feel betrayed and hurt. As a result, you lose all motivation and stay away from the relationship. This can cause you to become very distant from your partner since you act as if you no longer care about the relationship, which can make your partner feel they lost your interest, which can cause them to become very insecure about their role within the relationship.

The two of you end up withdrawing from each other and spending more time away than you do together. This can leave you feeling as if your partner no longer cares about the relationship, which makes it harder to continue being in it. Your partner may feel as if they are being abandoned by you and are unsure about their role in the relationship, which can make it easier for them to seek another partner who will give them more attention.

b. Beliefs

Anxiously preoccupied people who are insecure in their relationship tend to have the following beliefs about their partner:

i. "I can't count on them."

Someone with this attachment style will quickly believe they are not being treated fairly by their partner because they may experience feelings of helplessness and hopelessness in situations where their partner's behavior is not meeting their needs. This can cause them to see themselves as less than deserving of a relationship, making them more anxious about the relationship because they feel it is too good for them and will not work out for them.

This often leads to them believing that their partner will not value or love them in the same way they want to be loved, which causes them to focus on their partner's behavior while in the relationship. They will also see their partner as someone who is only there for themself and not for them, which causes them to become very mistrustful of their partner's motives.

This will lead to their partner working harder to regain their trust and prove they are worthy of the relationship. This will make their spouse believe they are making every effort to maintain the relationship. They may start trying to prove themself as worthy by being more romantic and intimate and giving more attention. During this time, the anxiously preoccupied person will have a negative reaction rather than a positive one, making them feel as if their partner does not care about them or is unwilling to work hard for the relationship.

ii. "I have to work harder on the relationship."

Someone with this attachment style will recognize they have to put more into the relationship to get the same out of it and will begin feeling as if they are doing all the work in the relationship without it being returned to them. They will also believe their partner does not do as much work in the relationship, which causes them to believe that they have to work harder to make up for this and be able to keep their partner interested.

This can cause them to feel as if the relationship is becoming too much work, and they have more on their hands than they can handle. This can then cause them to become overwhelmed by the amount of effort they are putting into the relationship, and they will feel it is too hard for them to handle for much longer without it affecting their health.

On the other hand, On the other hand, the partner will also notice this and wonder whether he/she is the only one who is really committed to the relationship, or will come to the conclusion that the relationship itself is simply too much for him/her which will cause them to become very insecure about their position. Partners of anxious people will begin feeling as if they are losing interest in the relationship This will make it easier for the person with anxious attachment to move on; in fact, he or she can start looking for another partner who, in his or her opinion, is more interested in making the relationship work.

This can make those with this attachment style feel as if they are not meeting their partner's needs and are unable to get ahead in the relationship. This can cause them to become very unhappy, and they will begin feeling as if the relationship is going downhill and find it difficult to recover. Their partner may notice this and feel they have made their partner feel neglected in the relationship, leading them to feel they are losing interest in the relationship and looking for another partner.

iii. "I don't matter to my partner."

Being in a relationship can be very hard on someone with this attachment style because they will begin to feel as if they cannot get what they need from their partner, which leaves them feeling as if they are constantly struggling to make the relationship work. This can cause them to think that their partner does not like them and is no longer interested in being with them, causing their partner to feel as if the relationship is not going in the direction they desire.

Their partner may then withdraw from the relationship, making the anxiously preoccupied person feel as if they are being abandoned; they will do anything to avoid this. During this time, their partner may feel that they are not able to reach their partner and get them to come back into the relationship, which can make them feel like they are out of touch with their partner and that their partner is no longer as interested in being with them.

This can cause those with this attachment style to start blaming themselves for what is happening between them, and they will begin feeling as if the relationship has no future or hope for success. They may then feel their partner does not care about them and will begin thinking about moving on with their life or start looking for another partner.

iv. "I am not good enough for my partner."

Their partner may begin to accept responsibility for their behavior, see that they are not satisfying the anxiously worried partner's needs, and resolve to do everything in their power to meet those needs. They will do this by trying to give them more attention and make the relationship a top priority for them, which can then cause the anxiously preoccupied person to have a negative response.

They will begin feeling as if they cannot get the attention they need to feel good about themselves and will have a negative reaction to this. This might draw attention to their partner, causing them to feel as though their needs are not being addressed, and they will begin to feel the relationship is no longer worthwhile. They may also begin focusing on other things that are important to them, like their profession or friends, which may cause their spouse to feel apprehensive about the relationship's future.

They do this to prevent their partner from leaving them and make them feel they are not as important to them. They can also start blaming themselves for their partner's lack of interest in the relationship, which can cause them to begin thinking about moving on or finding someone who is more interested in being with them.

These beliefs are often thought as good things, but they are not. When you have these beliefs, it will be very difficult for you to reach your full potential and achieve success in your relationship, and you will attempt to find someone else who is seeking these same things to make you happy. So, when they are put out of your life, it will be easier to find a partner who is also seeking these things and will make you happy, as opposed to trying to make your partner happy.

c. Confrontational Relationship.

Someone with this type of attachment style begins to distance themself from their partner when they begin fighting or have issues within the relationship. This is because they detest interacting and building relationships with antagonistic people. They will begin to treat their partner as if they are being confrontational with them and will distance themself from them to avoid letting their feelings escalate and becoming upset or angry, which can make it easier for them to end the relationship without feeling guilty about doing so, as, in their mind, it was all their partner's fault that the relationship ended.

For example...

Your partner becomes confrontational and loud when they begin to discuss things that are bothering or upsetting them within the relationship, which triggers your sensitive nature. You become defensive to prevent them from becoming louder and more confrontational with you as you begin to feel like you are being attacked. You begin to feel that your needs are not being met within the relationship and no longer feel you are important to your partner. You begin acting as if you do not need your partner anymore because they do not seem interested in what is bothering or upsetting you, and you become withdrawn from them in order to protect yourself from conflict.

The feelings of being attacked and not being listened to will make you feel as if you are no longer important to your partner, and you begin seeing them as a threat to your emotional well-being, which can cause you to become emotionally distant from them. You begin to act as if the relationship is over and distance yourself from them to avoid their confrontational nature. You will then find someone new who can make you feel as if you can continue being in the relationship without feeling any conflict, as in your mind, it does not matter what your partner has to say about anything.

d. No Glamorous Past.

Someone with this attachment style begins to distance themselves from their partner when they see nothing glamorous or exciting about the past or the relationship itself. They believe it is not worth being invested in a relationship like that, as they are not someone special or worth having enough time for. They will often act as if they no longer care about their partner when it comes to their past, making them feel like their partner does not care about them any longer, and making it easier for them to end the relationship without feeling guilty.

For example...

Your partner begins talking about their past and how great it was to be with someone who did not treat them the way you do. You start to doubt your place in the relationship because you feel like you are being compared to someone else. The thought of your partner wanting someone else will make you feel as if your relationship is no longer working out and that it is time for you to break up with them. You no longer see yourself being in the relationship and begin to feel there is no reason to stay in the relationship.

You feel you are being treated as less important because they are no longer wrapped up in the past, making you feel like you have no reason to be in the relationship any longer. The thought of staying in the relationship and fighting with your partner makes you feel as if you have no reason to stay together, which will make it easier for you to end the relationship to protect yourself from fighting or being ignored by them.

People with this type of attachment style will often become very dismissive toward their partner when they begin talking about past relationships, moments, or memories they had with other people. They will act as if they were never there or are no longer part of any of these relationships and stop listening to what their partner is saying. They tend to put their own feelings above everyone else's needs and start looking for someone new immediately.

Preoccupied anxious individuals are unreliable and unable to commit to a long-term relationship with someone who does not understand their anxieties. This is because they can become too panicky when their partner is trying to push them into a commitment, so they begin to get anxious and worried that they will not be able to handle it.

How you handle relationships is different from those with a secured attachment style. This is because of your sensitive nature and the way you always look for love when you can no longer be in a relationship that does not reciprocate your feelings. This is something that can be taken into consideration when beginning a new relationship with someone. You tend to become attached easily, which makes it important for anyone entering your life to take things slowly, as rushing you into anything will cause you to become frightened and uncomfortable and, in turn, push them away from wanting anything more from the relationship with you.

CHAPTER 5

RELATIONSHIP SUPERPOWERS OF ANXIOUS PREOCCUPIED ATTACHMENT

Having this type of attachment only sometimes means that all your relationships will end in a positive way. People with this attachment style have certain behaviors that make them very special in terms of relationships.

The following are some of the superpowers of the anxious preoccupied attachment style:

1. Committed to the Relationship

Anxious partners are usually committed to their relationship. They are unwilling to let things go without a fight and will never give up on a relationship unless it is over. This is because of the extreme anxiety they will feel if they are not with their partner. It is to the point that they will not have the ability to let go of this relationship and will act as if they are still in it. As long as they have someone they love, they will not be able to let them go or let them walk away.

How they show this behavior

a. Give up everything

Anxious partners will never give up on their partners. Even if they are being pushed away and left to feel as if they are nothing, they will still fight for them. They will do anything to get back into their lives and make them want to return to the relationship, as their anxiety cannot let go of the person they love. This behavior can make them seem desperate and needy and can often cause the other person in the relationship to push them away even more.

For example...

Your partner begins to ignore your attempt at communication, which causes you to act as if you are the only one who can save them from their loneliness. You believe your partner is not happy unless you are with them and that they will not be able to live without you, making it much easier for you to make things happen to get them back into your life.

You will often make excuses for their behavior, saying you understand why they need your presence in their life and that you can't leave them alone. This makes getting your partner back into a relationship easier than moving forward without them. You might even stop doing something else in your life to stay with them and help repair the damage that has been done. This can cause you to lose focus on your own goals and will make it more difficult for you to continue moving forward with your relationships.

While giving up everything is a great disadvantage, it can also serve as a superpower for you. No matter what happens in your relationship, you will always be able to come back and work things out. This allows you to repair any damage that has been done to the relationship and discover new situations that can benefit the two of you. Because of this superpower, for better or worse, things will never get boring or end without a fight.

It's important to remember that giving up your life and giving them all of your attention can be very overwhelming for both you and the other person in the relationship. You need a certain amount of independence and to ensure time is set aside for you and your partner. Allowing yourself to be so consumed by them could cause you to feel neglected and abandoned, which will create the urge for you to push them away.

b. Never let go of the relationship

Anxious partners can never truly let go of the relationship. Even if the relationship goes nowhere, they will continue to fight for the person they are with and will not accept being left behind. They refuse to believe that things are over and set a goal to bring him or her back into their lives so they can then continue in their search for someone else.

For example...

As you begin to end your relationship with your partner, you constantly hear them complaining that they feel abandoned and need you to be with them. This makes it hard for you to let go of the relationship. You keep jumping back into it and maintaining contact with the other person so that things will not be over between the two of you. You continue to tell your partner how they are still the one you love and that you need to be with them. This allows you to get them back into the relationship even if they do not want anything to do with it anymore. You are often focused on the other person and not on yourself. The only thing that you can make yourself think about is getting them back and often making excuses as to why they need to stay in your life. Even if you know it will be better for you if they are gone, you cannot stop thinking about them or your relationship.

The superpower in this is that you can keep fighting for the relationship. Even if things seem like they need to improve, you will continue trying to make them work. If there is still a chance of saving the relationship, you will stand by their side and help them fix the wrong things. You will not give up on the relationship and always hope that one day, everything will change and work out between the two of you.

While this behavior can be helpful in some situations, it can also cause you to have a harder time moving forward from any negative experience that comes from it. This is because you are never going to see anything good in losing someone who was once so important in your life. You will always be thinking about them and how they were the only person you could ever love. This causes you to be overprotective of your feelings and to continue giving them as much attention as possible.

c. Never move on

Anxious partners refuse to let go of the past, even if it is no longer in their control. They will let old patterns continue and can have trouble moving forward with their lives, which often turns into depression. They will often struggle with loving someone else again and will be stuck in a cycle of not being able to move on from a certain past relationship.

For example...

Once you decide that you want to get rid of your partner, you begin to feel as if everything you do is for them. You feel as if all your time and energy are being used to make them come back into your life. You continue to obsess over them and refuse to move on, which will cause you to have a hard time finding someone else you can give your attention to. You cannot allow yourself to go out on your own or meet new people without fearing that it will be with them. This creates a pattern that your partner is used to and that they are not going to be able to move forward without you.

The superpowers in this are that you are able to keep thinking about them and the relationship, even after it has been over for some time. You will still be able to keep their memory alive, which will make it easier for you to try and get them back into your life. The way that you continue fighting for the relationship is what makes this behavior so much of a benefit to you. You are never going to be able to let go of the past and will always be thinking about the person. You will always have this one person that is still very special to you, and the only thing that you can think about will be them. The actions that come from this are often very selfish, but they serve a purpose in your life; they keep you happy and allow you to keep a new relationship alive as long as you need to.

While it is not necessary for you to move on from the past, you need to learn how to get yourself out of this rut. You have to make sure you can balance your life between the relationship and that they do not completely take over who you are. If it is not possible to balance these two things, consider getting some help from a professional counselor.

This superpower in someone with this attachment style is very helpful in keeping you happy and allowing you to keep a relationship alive. You can do anything to get your partner back into your life and will always be thinking about how they are the only one who can make you feel good. This is important because it allows you to continue believing that love is possible and not just something that happens by chance. If it was not for how this superpower has affected you, you might not have been able to keep having hope that you will one day find someone willing to keep fighting for the relationship. You are able to spread happiness throughout your life, which is what keeps these feelings of attachment and hope possible. If it was not for your ability to continue these relationships, you might not be able to get yourself out of them and move forward with your life.

Being able to cling to someone and fight for them is often a good thing because it makes us realize that there is more out there. It allows us to hope that we will meet someone willing to put up a fight like we have been doing with each other. This can cause us to see the potential in other people because we can see how much someone is willing to care about us. However, you have also been giving this behavior a power that is out of control and resistant to change. If you have been relying on it too much, it may be time to start trying something new that allows you more freedom to move forward with life.

2. Highly Attuned to Their Partner's Needs

Another superpower of people with this attachment style is finding their partner's needs and responding to them accordingly. Because they are trying to make their partner want them, they will always pay close attention to what their partner wants and needs. This is because they realize that their partner would not be with them if they weren't liked and wanted, so they will always do anything to figure out what is necessary in order to keep the relationship going.

How they show this behavior

a. Sensitivity

Anxious partners are always sensitive to their partner's needs and will let their partner know what they are feeling in a way that shows how much they care about them. This can make their partner feel as if they actually matter and is an advantage for all anxious types. They will respond to anything going on in the other person's life, even if it is not something they should be responding to. This gives them great insight into how to make everything better, especially when they suddenly realize that their partner seems unhappy and needs some extra attention to bring them back into the relationship.

For example...

Your partner begins to act differently and seems as if they do not want to be with you. They begin saying they are unhappy and don't feel the same way about you anymore. Because you are so infatuated with them, you begin to inquire about their mental state. In doing this, you realize there is something going on with them outside of your relationship, which causes you to become sensitive to what they might be feeling. You know they need someone who can make things better for them and will make sure they know that whatever it is that's making them unhappy will be fixed as long as you are together.

So, if you see your partner acting in a way that makes you concerned about them, it is important for you to let them know. This will allow them to feel as if they are actually being heard and loved by someone, which is a major advantage for anxious types. It also allows them to realize that this behavior or situation can be changed and is not something big that needs to be fixed permanently. They are able to realize that it is just something that was an inconvenience and will be fixed as soon as it happens again.

It is important to be considerate of your partner's needs, but it is also crucial not to take over their life. You must ensure that you are able to continue doing things that are important to you and that you do not completely alter your identity to make them happy. If it becomes something that is making you unsure about who you want to be, it might be time for you to stop focusing all of your attention on them and start focusing some on yourself as well. If your partner still feels the same way about you after you have done this, it might mean that they want to see everyone happy, and they don't mind making other people happy.

b. Supportiveness

Anxious partners are always there to support their partners through all situations they might be going through. They will be there to listen and reassure them that everything is going to be okay, even if it doesn't seem like it at the time. This is because they want their partner to feel loved and wanted, so they will do whatever it takes for them to feel secure about their relationship.

For example...

Your partner has been experiencing some issues with their job, which causes them to become stressed and afraid that they might lose their job. You don't know what is going on with them, but you know they are not acting normally. In a situation like this, you might be unsure if you should say anything or just let it go. You know they are dealing with something big and don't want to add to their worries by being too sensitive and asking them questions about what is happening. You recognize that the best course of action is to be there for them and ensure they feel wanted and needed. So, you will make sure your schedule has room for them at any point in time, and if something comes up, you will adjust whatever plans you have made in order for them to feel comfortable going through this situation that they are experiencing.

This type of behavior is crucial in relationships. It shows you are able to be there for someone no matter what and will never let them feel as if they don't matter to you. This is why it is such an amazing advantage to anxious types and something they should always be working on. They need to make sure that they are showing support to the people who are closest to them, so they know how much they mean to someone. This can be difficult because everyone goes through very hard and trivial situations in their life and cannot always depend on the people closest to them to be there. Supporting others requires a great deal of time and effort, which gives them the impression that someone will always be there for them.

It is important to put other people's needs before your own only sometimes. While you will always try to make sure that the people closest to you know that they are loved, it is important for you to understand that sometimes, you need to be there for yourself instead of doing everything for someone else. If your partner is not able to acknowledge how much they mean to you, it might be time for you to take a step back from this relationship and focus on yourself instead of the two of you together. If you do not know what to do in this situation, you should seek help.

c. Responsibility

Anxious partners can take on the responsibilities of their relationships easily. They are comfortable taking the initiative and doing whatever is necessary to ensure the success of their relationship. This can be very beneficial in a relationship because they know they can handle things the way they need to.

For example...

You are aware that your partner has had a difficult day, but you do not know why. Considering things have been going great for them lately, and this is the first thing you hear about, it is important for you to make sure that things are okay before you start worrying about what could be happening to them. So, you let your partner know they can come to you if they need anything and be there for them in the way they need. They realize nothing has really changed between the two of you, and everything will still go smoothly as long as they have someone there for them when they need help. You take the lead and show them you will always be there for them no matter what, which is something anxious types always have a problem doing.

How someone acts in their relationships can affect the outcome of their relationships with others. Anxious partners are incredibly conscientious individuals who make every effort to ensure their lives run smoothly. They will always act this way because it is important for them to know they won't have problems with anything when dealing with it on their own. If you want your relationships to be successful, this is a quality you should constantly work on.

While it is never a good idea to take things into your own hands because you are afraid of other people's reactions, it is important to realize that sometimes they must be considered. Your partner cannot always make sure that you know how they feel, especially in cases where their feelings are very deeply buried due to their anxiety disorder. Sometimes this means that you should be the one who manages the relationship and does everything for them instead of letting them do it on their own. An anxious partner will not be able to understand the difference between doing things on your own or taking the initiative because they want someone else to make sure that everything works out well for them.

This superpower is often hard for an anxious partner to fully utilize. It requires them to be in the spotlight and be aware of how the people around them are feeling. They must understand that it is not always about themselves but also the people they care about and love. Being able to make sure that the people you are closest to know how much you care about them is a very powerful thing, which can cause someone to go above and beyond just for their significant other. This superpower allows anxious types to show their care for other people through action instead of just saying how much they love someone.

3. Help Partners to See Themselves Positively

Another superpower that anxious types have is the ability to make sure their significant other sees the good in them. This means they can help their partner see themselves in a positive light and know they are good enough for them. Even at the expense of their own happiness, anxious types will always be able to make sure that the people closest to them have a positive outlook about them, their life and what they have been through.

How they show this behavior

a. Excuse others when they're wrong

This attachment pattern tends to have them see their partner as perfect, and they will forgive them for their mistakes. This can be seen in situations of infidelity or other negative behavior that occurs in a relationship, resulting in the anxious preoccupied person feeling too happy to see any flaws with their partner, which could leave the partner feeling validated that they are good enough and don't need to change a thing.

For example...

You might continuously overlook your partner's mistakes, even if you already know they're wrong. You may continue to have a favorable opinion of them despite knowing they are not perfect and have a few flaws. If your partner commits a transgression, you are willing to forgive them because you love them so much, and this is the only way you can comprehend why they would do such a thing, even though it makes no sense to anyone else. You might not be able to accept their mistakes for too long without trying to find a way for the two of you to fix what was wrong so that the relationship can continue normally. This shows that anxious individuals will always see the good in the people they love, even if it causes them to be unhappy.

This characteristic greatly affects relationships. It shows that although the anxious partner genuinely cares about other people, they will always put their own feelings and emotions before anyone else's. They want to make sure that everyone around them has a positive outlook on the world and will try their hardest to ensure that they always think positively.

But this can also cause problems in a relationship. Anxious partners will not be able to understand why their partner would be so negative about the truly important moments. They won't understand why anyone would be upset in the moments when they should be feeling happy and loved. This can cause people to feel misunderstood by anxious individuals, which causes couples problems when they cannot accept their partner for who they are and act accordingly.

b. Avoid rejecting or distancing themselves

For an anxiously attached person, saying "no" to their partner can be difficult, and it may not come out very easily. This is because people who are anxious preoccupied will be uncomfortable with the idea of saying "no" to their partner, as they want to make sure that the other person has a good outlook on life and does not feel sad in any way. This can result in their partner feeling like they cannot get their needs and wants in their relationship, which will cause them to feel very sad and angry.

For example...

When your partner needs something or asks for a favor, you make sure to fulfill it because you do not want to upset them. You might be more willing to oblige with their request because you do not want them to feel sad about anything. You might be afraid of saying "no" because you know they will not react well to that, and it will cause them to have a negative outlook on their life. You do not want them to feel bad about anything, so you make sure to indulge in their request instead of respectfully declining.

This superpower can help your relationship by ensuring that your partner is happy and enjoys doing what they do in life. It can also prevent arguments by ensuring your significant other always has a positive mindset. But it can also cause problems if your partner cannot get what they want from you, which may make them feel as if you do not care about or respect them. If one partner is unwilling to make improvements, this could result in the breakdown of a relationship, and it can be extremely painful if a person is unable to be honest with their partner.

Continually putting yourself in a position where you feel used or taken advantage of will make you very unhappy. Your partner will continually take advantage of your selflessness until it is too late, and you will feel that you can never adequately communicate your needs. You may start to feel like everyone around you is using or abusing your kindness, which may result in an argument that leaves both individuals feeling bad about themselves.

c. Excuse themselves when they're wrong

Similarly to how an anxious preoccupied person excuses others when they make a mistake, they will often excuse themselves for the mistake and try to figure out how it's their problem and not their partner's. When problems occur in the relationship, the anxious partner will attempt to make it seem like it is their fault and feel bad about what happened. This can lead to avoiding any serious problems in their relationship because they are afraid they will face rejection or disappointment from their partner if they do anything wrong.

For example...

You might continually blame yourself for making a mistake in your relationship and feel really bad about it. You may feel like you don't deserve to be with someone so perfect, which makes you want to distance yourself from them because they are the only thing keeping you going. You might try not to make a mistake because the relationship would end if it happened again, and your partner wouldn't be able to accept it. You will feel so bad about yourself and the things you have done that you might not even be able to stand the person you love anymore.

This behavior can help a relationship by allowing your partner to forgive any mistakes you make. It can also allow you to accept the things that your significant other has done because they will already feel bad about it. This can encourage them to do better, and it will also allow you to feel secure in the relationship because their perfectness won't be threatened if they see that your imperfections don't matter because you love them for who they are.

But, constantly focusing on how much of a mistake you made and how bad of a person you are for what happened may cause problems with your relationship, especially if your partner is tired of hearing about it every time something goes wrong. This may cause your partner to lose interest in the relationship if they feel they are not appreciated or accepted for who they are. It can also lead to an inability to gracefully accept your mistakes, which could lead to the end of a relationship if one person cannot accept their partner for who they are.

A person with this attachment style can effectively assist their partner in seeing themselves in a positive light. This helps them show their feelings towards anyone that is important to them and allows them to feel more in tune with their partner's needs and wants. They will never be afraid to help their partner through a rough time, as they know their happiness is more important than anything else.

While this superpower is great and can help couples understand each other better, it can also cause problems. People do not like feeling used or taken advantage of in any way, and if they cannot get their needs met by someone, they will feel very frustrated. This feeling can cause you to feel sad that you are unable to support their loved one's needs, which may cause both individuals to start arguing more than normal.

The superpowers of someone with this attachment style can either be a strength to their relationship or a weakness. If used positively, they can help strengthen a relationship and make one feel more in tune with their significant other's needs and wants. However, if not utilized properly, these superpowers can cause problems in their relationship.

CHAPTER 6

THINGS TO REMEMBER WHEN LOVING

Loving someone can be challenging at times. Your attachment style will greatly affect how you treat and handle your partner. The way you express and show your feelings for them will also have an impact on them. Therefore, it is essential to understand that there are certain considerations to make when loving someone.

When loving someone, there are things to remember, such as:

1. Be willing to allow your partner to love you back.

When we focus only on ourselves and do not give our partner time to love us, it makes it more difficult for the couple to function, which causes the relationship to become strained and uncomfortable for both of us. This can lead one or both to feel frustrated and worried about the relationship. one should age dialogue in the couple, listening to what the other is feeling within the relationship. In this way it is easier for both of you to understand and work on your relationship since you will be less stressed and there will be fewer misunderstandings.

There are actions you can take to encourage your partner to return your affection, such as:

a. Allow them to be there for you when you are feeling down.

When feeling down or in need of someone to talk to or confide in, you allow your partner to be there for you and listen to what is bothering or upsetting you. This can make the process of being in the relationship easier and give both of you comfort while being able to speak freely without feeling as if anyone is listening or judging what you have to say. The person being listened to will have been heard and will not feel that they are bothering their partner and can end up staying close to that person without having any issues of them overreacting or becoming upset about anything that was said.

It simply means that they are willing to be there when you need them, making it easier for both of you to be in a relationship without feeling like your partner does not understand or care about who you are. This does not imply that your partner must always be available to assist you in times of need.

b. Let your partner show you that they love you.

When your partner shows their love for you, you will see how much they truly care for you and are willing to be there for you in any situation without being judgmental or critical. This can make the relationship more comfortable for both of you, making it easier to communicate with one another on a deeper level. Additionally, you will see how committed they are to the connection, making it easier for you to have faith in them. You'll also be able to express your love for them without worrying that you are betraying them in any way.

This does not mean that your partner is demonstrating their love for you or that they care about you; it just means that they will stop at nothing to keep the relationship healthy and secure without ever abusing or hurting you in any way. This allows both of you to feel as if you have a lot more trust within the relationship and that your partner is willing to accept anything that may go wrong between the two of you and will not take advantage of each other in any way. Trust is something that will take time for both of you to build up, which should never be taken for granted by either party. If it is, it will cause issues within the relationship between the two of you, and you will never feel as if you have the things that you need within the relationship.

c. Let your partner understand how they make you feel.

When your partner understands why and how they are making you feel the way they are, it can give them a better understanding of why and how they are doing things in a certain manner without making it seem as if anything is wrong. This allows for a more comfortable relationship for both of you, which allows either one of you to grow closer to the other and find comfort in everything that is going on between the two of you and within the relationship.

This is something that most people do not always realize they should do when they are in a relationship, thinking that they are never going to have any issues with their partner because of this, which can cause them to become very irritated at times with their partner because of how things happen within the relationship without ever understanding why or how one thing is happening in a certain way.

d. Allow your partner to talk about any personal issues that they may have with you.

As the relationship develops and grows stronger, it can help your partner understand why something happened in a certain way without them taking advantage of things and without it being clear as too what has been happening. When your partner is honest with you about their personal issues with you and how they feel, it can help them gain a better understanding of how they are doing things in ways that may not initially appear right or wrong.

The more comfortable the relationship between the two of you becomes, the more your partner will be willing to accept things that are going on within the relationship, as well as be able to let go of a few personal issues that they hold onto, which will allow you to grow closer in many ways.

The more comfortable the relationship becomes, the more either one of you can talk about anything that is going on within the relationship and how it feels, allowing you to understand one another.

Letting your partner know how they are making you feel is something that can cause your partner to misunderstand why and how they are making you feel within the relationship without allowing either one of you to have any issues within the relationship. The more comfortable the relationship becomes, it will allow both of you to become more honest and understanding without having any issues with each other, and it will allow both of you to grow closer in many ways.

2. Let your partner know how much you love them.

When your partner knows that you truly love them, it can make them feel as if you care about them and will not take advantage of any situation that may arise within the relationship. This creates a level of trust between the two of you that makes it easier for you to be open and honest with one other without being critical or judgmental. The more you can express love for your partner, the more they will feel confident in their relationship with you and not have any issues with things that are going on within the relationship.

When your partner feels as if they have a lot more trust within the relationship, it allows them to let go of a few things they hold onto in their mind that they think they cannot let go of, and this can cause both of you to grow closer.

There are actions you can take to demonstrate your love for your partner, such as:

a. Show them how much you care about what is going on within the relationship.

When you can show your partner that you care about what is going on between the two of you, it can help them feel as if they can trust you in a way they have never felt before. This means that they will not be afraid of how things may turn out with either one of you within the relationship, and things will happen without them being afraid in any way.

You can do things like:

- Be there for your partner when they need you.
- Be a good listener for your partner and demonstrate that you are paying attention by avoiding all forms of distraction.
- Focus on the things that your partner is saying and try to respond to what they are saying in a way that will show you care about how they feel.
- Appreciate the things that your partner does for you, no matter how small or big they may be.
- Let your partner know that you appreciate everything they do for you and will continue to do so in the future. You can say things like: "**Thank you so much; I love it when you do this for me,**" or "**You are so great; I am so glad that we are doing this together.**"
- Be honest with your partner and let them know how you feel. If you are being told something that upsets you, express your feelings to your partner by saying things like: "**This hurts me because of...**"

It does not imply that you must do anything specific with your partner, but you should express how you feel about the relationship's current state. You should not be afraid, and do not take anything personally because your partner's feelings will start to become more authentic and honest with you. Let them know you are there for them whenever they need it.

b. Take time in your relationship to make each other feel special.

When you take time in your relationship to make each other feel special, you can allow the other person to express himself in a way that will help him to be more open about his feelings and how he feels about things that happen within the relationship. In fact, when you are confident about your partner's feelings, you are not afraid to either ask or answer.. The more comfortable the relationship becomes, the more your partner will be able to open up about things happening within the relationship and let go of a few personal issues because of how you treat them within the relationship.

You can do things within your relationship, such as:

- Be there for your partner when they need you most and show them that you are a good listener.

- Get to know your partner's likes and dislikes and make sure to do things for them, such as buying them little gifts just to let them know that you appreciate everything they do for you.

- Surprise your partner with something special from time to time without letting them know what it is beforehand.

- Communicate to your partner that they are an integral part of your life.

- Show your partner that you care about them by saying things like: **"I love how persistent you are,"** **"I appreciate how you are with me,"** or **"You are so great at doing this; I**

really enjoy it."

- Acknowledge their efforts and express your appreciation for everything they do for you.

- Be genuine and honest with your partner by telling them what is on your mind, even if it is something small or big.

This is when your partner will start to have a lot more trust in you, and they can also start to let go of a few feelings that they have been holding onto because of how you treat them.

c. Give your partner time and space to do whatever it is that they want to do.

When you give your partner time and space, it allows their feelings about you not being around to change for the better, as opposed to feeling as if something is wrong with them because they are not over their previous relationships or other such things. As your partner starts to be more honest with you about their feelings, it can help them let go of the things they have been holding onto in the past, and it will allow them to start trusting you with everything they are thinking and doing without feeling as if there is something wrong or different about them.

You can do things like:

- Don't interfere with your partner's plans to do something fun or spend time with their family and friends.

- Let your partner know that you trust them with everything

they do and will be there for them whenever they need it.

- Let them know if there is anything that you can do to help, , and if there is nothing at all, then tell them that as well.
- Respect your partner's decisions and choices in life.
- When you respect your partner's decisions and choices, it can allow them to do the things they want without feeling as if they have to check with you before doing so.
- Give your partner space when they need it the most and let them know if there is anything that you can do,

This can help build a stronger bond between you and your partner as they will be able to open up more and let go of a few things they have been holding onto from their past, allowing them to feel more comfortable with the relationship.

d. Be honest and trustworthy with your partner in every way possible.

When you are honest and trustworthy with your partner, it allows them to trust you a lot more, which will help build a stronger bond between the two of you. You should be honest in how you talk to your partner and let them know how you feel about things. It is something they will appreciate, and it will help you build a stronger bond with them. It will help if you honestly care about your partner's feelings and always help them out with what they need.

You can do things like:

- Always be honest with your partner, and if they ask you a

question for which you do not have the answer, let them know so they can seek your help.

- Be there for your partner whenever they need you the most and be willing to help them out in any way possible.
- If there is something going on in your relationship or anything bothering you, let your partner know about it so they can try to fix it for you.
- Be upfront with your feelings about things that are happening within the relationship.
- Let your partner know that you will always tell them what is going on for you and that you will try to help them out with whatever it is they are going through.
- If there is something your partner needs, tell them you will try to help them in any way possible.
- Talk to your partner about the issues you have within the relationship and see how they can help you.
- If issues are going on within the relationship, tell your partner and work together to solve it as adults instead of keeping it inside or ignoring them without seriously talking about it.
- If you are going through something your partner does not know about, be open with them and tell them so they can help you.
- Be willing to compromise on things and let your partner

know what is important to you.

- Let your partner know that what is happening in their life is very important to you because it is.
- Give your partner a voice in how the household is run; they'll feel more at ease knowing how much you value them and can make decisions without constantly seeking your advice or suggestions.

Knowing when it is time to apologize and when it is not can help you and your partner have much more trust in each other. This can strengthen your relationship and give you confidence that they will be there for you no matter what happens in daily life. It will also help the two of you to feel as if you are starting over together, so that way, the future of your relationship will last longer than ever before. This will also bring the two of you closer together and allow you to have a long-term relationship that is filled with happiness, love, and trust.

e. Find out what your partner is looking for in the relationship, then do it.

When you are aware of your partner's desires for the relationship, it is easier to help them feel as if you and they are on the same wavelength . This will help them trust you and stop feeling lonely or out of place.

This will also allow them to find happiness within their relationship and be happy and appreciated by you. Knowing what your partner is looking for within the relationship can make it easier for them to feel like things are moving forward instead of dragging on because they may be looking for something that you may not be able to give or do.

You can do things like:

- Talk about how important this person is in your partner's life.
- Take the time to explain what they mean to you and what they mean in your life.
- Tell them how much they mean to you and that losing them would be one of the worst things you can imagine.
- Be available for your partner to discuss any issues or problems that may be bothering them.
- Be understanding when it comes to your partner's situation in life, and let them know that if they have any issues or problems, they can talk to you about it.
- Show your partner that things like this matter a lot more to you than most would think.
- Talk to your partner about what is going on within the relationship.
- Take the time to explain how important this person is in your partner's life so what they mean to them becomes clear.
- Make sure you tell them how much you care about this person and show it through action rather than words.
- Let your partner know that if anything ever happens in their life, you will be by their side. Don't hesitate to tell

them how important they are to you because reassurance, especially when unsolicited, is much more important than you might think,in building trust.If your partner is going through something, talk to them about it and reassure them that you will be there for them no matter what happens because you care about their feelings as much as you care about what they mean to you.

Knowing how to be there for your partner will help them feel like they are with someone who cares about them, and it makes it easier for them to know that you care about what is going on in their life. This will allow you to build stronger feelings together and for the two of you to have a close bond.

3. Love yourself

To be able to love others, the most important thing you can do is to love yourself. If you do not love yourself, that means you will never be able to place any affection on anyone else because you will always be too focused on trying to make yourself happy and make sure that you are always satisfied in life.

If you love yourself for the person you are, it will allow your partner to have more trust in you and know that there is no reason for them to doubt anything that comes from your mouth. When your partner knows that you love them, they will feel that nothing is more important than how they feel when they are with you, and it will be easier for them to put their trust in what may result from talking to someone who cares about them.

Many people may think that love should always mean that you put other people's feelings first within a relationship, but if you do not love yourself and focus on making yourself happy, then your partner will not feel the same way about you and the bond that is shared between the both of you will start to weaken from there on out.

Loving yourself allows your partner to know that you are happy with who they are, what they do for a living, and how things are coming up in their life without being scared to death of what is going on because they know that everything is going to be all right.

4. Give respect.

Give your partner the same amount of respect that you would want in return. If you do not give your partner respect, then they will not feel as if there is a reason for them to put trust into what you may say or do because they know you do not care about what goes on within their life and how they feel about it.

Many people will say there are things going on in their life that make it hard for them to understand why the other person cannot love them the same way they are supposed to be loved. If you do not respect what they are going through in their life, then they will feel as if there is no reason for them to trust the way you speak about the things that are bothering them.

Love is found in the heart of all people. Love is not always represented by how long a person has been with someone, how much money they are making, or how many friends they have in their life. Love is represented by how you treat the other person and yourself inside and outside your relationship.

CHAPTER 7

THE EFFECT OF ANXIOUS PREOCCUPIED ATTACHMENT ON PROFESSIONAL RELATIONSHIPS

Your attachment style can greatly affect how you work with others or in a professional setting.

HOW ANXIOUS-PREOCCUPIED PRESENT THEIR WORK RELATIONSHIPS

The following is how someone with an anxious preoccupied attachment style presents themselves professionally:

1. Overly Analyse Criticism or Feedback

Anxious preoccupied individuals may be concerned that the "hidden meaning behind critical feedback" or the "over-personalization of constructive criticism" indicates a lack of value or worth. Similarly, they may misinterpret delays in response from their supervisor or coworkers as rejection, thereby increasing anxiety and decreasing productivity.

What triggers this behavior?

a. Unclear communication

Those with an anxious preoccupied attachment style tend to be very nervous when communicating with their superiors or colleagues. Some say they need to overcommunicate certain information to "empower" themselves, while others cannot express their thoughts and ideas properly. This can lead to them making many mistakes when communicating, not because they are incompetent but because they have a lot of anxiety surrounding communication.

For example...

You might feel like you constantly have to explain yourself when you make a mistake or get feedback, even though your coworkers clearly communicated the message. While it may seem like these misunderstandings and miscommunications are just a small thing to worry about, they can affect your professional relationships. This anxiety can make you less confident in the workplace and keep you from expressing yourself clearly.

As a result, you will try to mask your anxiety by over-communicating information to others or by being timider and avoiding feedback.

While this strategy may initially seem successful, over time, it can create more problems within the workplace. When you are unsure of whether something is wrong with your job performance, for instance, you will be reluctant to share your thoughts and ideas with others. This can irritate the people around you about constantly explaining themselves for your sake. For everyone to feel comfortable in a working environment where employees properly express their thoughts and ideas, all employees must be able to share their opinions and work collaboratively with others comfortably.

It would help if you considered that all of your coworkers, superiors, and subordinates are human beings and deserve to be treated with respect and honesty. A workplace where employees are constantly apprehensive about expressing their opinions and ideas is not productive. Like in romantic relationships, the more anxious you become about your coworkers' feedback or communication style, the more likely you will misinterpret these traits as an indication of their unhappiness with you or their lack of value for you.

b. Prior Inconsistencies

Those with an anxious preoccupied attachment style tend to be prone to inconsistency in their work. They may need to think things through or try coming up with ideas on the go without proper preparation or planning. This leads to them presenting work that doesn't match the standards they set for themselves at first. When this fails to gain their colleague's approval, they become nervous and perceive the situation as a threat. This may cause them to become overly cautious and excessively critical of their own work.

For example...

While you may have tried your best to achieve a certain standard with regard to work quality, this may need to be more organized when it is presented to others. You might become so nervous about this situation that you completely avoid sharing your work or ideas with others. Instead of learning from your errors and moving forward with your career, you will likely spend a great deal of time attempting to "fix" them.

As a result, your coworkers and superiors will overlook your quality work and instead focus on your mistakes. You will feel like you have to "prove yourself" more than ever to please the people around you. Suppose you are constantly worrying about whether or not you will be able to do a good job for others. It can be extremely challenging to think clearly about professional challenges and opportunities in such a case. You will often be too nervous to accurately assess your performance and come up with the best course of action for yourself.

There are numerous possible causes for your inconsistency in thought, over-analyzation, and general anxiety about ideas at work, but it is essential that you realize you are not alone. Many of your coworkers and supervisors are probably experiencing similar feelings of anxiety and annoyance when sharing ideas and communicating with their superiors.

c. Lack of Practical Experience

Those with this attachment style often need more practical experience. They may be unwilling to put themselves out there and gain valuable experience that could give them an edge in the future. This causes them to underestimate the value or usefulness of their work, which can lead them to exaggerate the things they will negatively hear from their superiors. They may even become more shut-in and avoid communication altogether.

For example...

You may feel like you must go above and beyond your work to prove yourself as "worthy enough" of the praise that those around you give out sparingly. You might be so nervous about this constant need for approval from the people around you that you avoid doing anything that could lead to failure or rejection. This results in you needing to gain experience or understanding of what it is like to work in that particular field and, therefore, being unable to adapt to it in the future.

Over time, this can lead to you feeling more and more nervous about doing something new that could lead to failure because you do not understand the consequences of failure in your field, thus avoiding many opportunities to get ahead in your field. Furthermore, when you are constantly seeking the approval of others, you will become increasingly passive-aggressive with yourself and the people around you. This makes it difficult for others to trust your opinions or thoughts on certain situations, as they may lack confidence that you are expressing your true feelings.

As you overanalyze their criticism or feedback, you will begin to come across as more and more pretentious in your opinions and thoughts. This may cause friction between you and your superiors or colleagues as they begin to trust your opinions less and less. In some cases, this can even irritate the people around you because they must constantly repeat themselves when explaining the required work. This can make it difficult for others to trust your decisions in certain situations, especially considering that a lack of trust is one of the primary causes of problems in professional relationships.

d. Too Much of a Perfectionist

Those with an anxious preoccupied attachment style tend to take criticism personally because they fear it indicates a lack of value or worth. Instead of addressing this as a learning experience that could help them improve their skills, talent, or productivity in the future, these individuals may be too anxious to accept feedback and are overprotective of their identities. Since they feel so much pressure to live up to their own ideal self-image and of others' opinions about them, they may become more obsessive about their work and perfectionism.

For example...

You might take feedback and communication very personally, feeling like you are harshly criticized, when in reality, the feedback is constructive and meant to help you improve your performance. Instead of seeing this as an opportunity to grow and become a more effective employee, you might be too anxious to accept the criticism—even if your superior cares about your growth and success.

You tend to do everything perfectly to avoid criticism or mistakes. When everyone around you can understand this perfectionist attitude of yours, they may be understanding of your anxieties. However, when others are unable to understand why you are so afraid of making mistakes, they might think you are irrational or have an inflated ego.

Because of this, you will tend to work more slowly and become less productive. This is because you are more anxious about making mistakes, making it harder to concentrate on your work. Conversations can take longer, as you may become more hesitant to speak and less open to receiving feedback from others.

You tend to overanalyze criticisms or feedback because you see them as a reflection of your current self-worth. This is the anxiety you feel when other people notice a flaw in you, which makes you want to change it immediately rather than consider it as an opportunity to grow. You may become passive-aggressive toward the people around you and be unable to respect their opinions or thoughts.

As a result, you will tend to avoid communication to prevent any negative thoughts from others that could cause you to feel like a failure. But given that a lack of trust is one of the main reasons for issues in business relationships, this will only make it harder for others to believe in your judgment in certain situations.

2. Struggle With Work-Related Anxiety

Anxious-preoccupied individuals may be concerned that they are not up to the tasks at hand. In a professional setting, they may be worried that they cannot handle the work or that their supervisor will think poorly of them. Consequently, to protect themselves from these perceived inadequacies, anxious preoccupied individuals may isolate themselves from others and become overly defensive when criticisms arise.

What triggers this behavior?

a. Initially Overwhelmed

Anxious preoccupied individuals can initially find themselves overwhelmed by the amount of work they have to do or the number of resources they are given. This can lead some to isolate themselves from others, not wanting to draw the attention of those around them. They may also take on whichever tasks others find less desirable and become resentful about having to complete these difficult or unwanted tasks.

For example...

There is a lot of pressure to finish this project on time. You are used to preparing your presentations, but you are given these slides to hand out at a conference in a short period of time. While you were once able to prepare these presentations easily, you feel so overwhelmed by the tasks given to you that your anxiety increases, and you are unable to complete them on time.

Anxious preoccupied individuals may also be caught off guard when overwhelmed with work or when having their opinions ignored. They may need more social support from others and may avoid asking for help from their boss for fear of being undermined or criticized. In this case, they may hesitate to ask for clarification in their work.

As a result, they may struggle to get into the groove of things and may find themselves being overly defensive in response to a query from a client or colleague. They are likely to feel that their opinions or work style is important and will fight any suggestions that contradict their opinion about the task. Even when their opinion is incorrect, they will not want to admit it because they want to avoid paying attention to the fact that their work style or job performance needs improvement.

It would help if you considered your own emotional capacity and what you can realistically handle. There's no denying there is a lot of pressure in the workplace, and everyone occasionally gets overwhelmed. Many bosses are willing to help you out when you are clearly struggling with some aspect of your job, so don't feel it's necessary to isolate yourself or become defensive to protect yourself from criticism.

b. Fear of Being Ignored or Underestimated

Anxious preoccupied individuals are often afraid that others will ignore them or not recognize their efforts. They may also believe that others around them think less of their productivity and talent, even if these coworkers have never mentioned this. To protect themselves from these perceived inadequacies, anxious preoccupied individuals may isolate themselves from others and become overly defensive when criticisms arise. The idea that they are being ignored or underestimated often causes them to feel like they will be safer if they spend less time around other people.

For example...

You have been given a large number of files to organize, and you are feeling overwhelmed. Although you are not the kind of person who likes to solicit assistance, you are aware that all your coworkers are capable of efficiently organizing files. However, you are afraid that no one will think of you when they are asked to help with this task. You spend more time alone at your desk and less time in the meeting room with colleagues, further isolating yourself from others.

But given that a lack of trust is one of the main reasons for issues in business relationships, this will only make it harder for others to believe in your judgment in certain situations. You decide to catch up on the files you have been neglecting and avoid having them fall through the cracks again by focusing more on this task than others. This will show that you are more dedicated to your job and will send a message to your boss that you don't need constant attention or help.

Anxious preoccupied individuals can be very critical of themselves, so they must recognize their strengths and areas for improvement for them to grow professionally. If you are anxious preoccupied, it is sometimes necessary to remind yourself of the positive qualities you bring to your job, even if others don't appreciate them as much as you do. Consider taking an inventory of your strengths and comparing them with others' weaknesses to remind yourself that you are a valuable employee.

c. Fear of Disapproval

Anxious preoccupied individuals may fear disapproval from others when they speak up in a professional setting. They may fear their ideas will be ignored, criticized, or not accepted by their superiors, peers, and subordinates. Furthermore, they believe this disapproval, criticism, and rejection will happen even if they are 100% correct. Since they tend to want approval from others and internally worry about what others think of them, this would result in further anxiety for the individual.

For example...

You are planning a meeting for everyone to attend. However, you are feeling overwhelmed with all the logistical details. You have been assigned close to 100 tasks that need to be completed, but it seems like there needs to be an end in sight. You fear you will be viewed as incompetent if you say anything to anyone, so you remain silent and concentrate on doing your work alone. Even though your boss has asked you multiple times to help with various aspects of this project, you avoid telling them what you need to finish it on time because you fear they will reject your requests.

This would result in a domino effect. The project could have been more successful than it was, and your boss would also be unhappy with your performance. This may result in an overall poor performance appraisal and possible rejection from the company. You decide to check in with your boss and tell them exactly what you need in order to finish the project by the end of the week. They are happy with your request and happy that you knew to ask for help so you could meet all your deadlines.

When anxious preoccupied individuals fear disapproval from others, it usually means they need approval to feel good about themselves. As a result, they seek approval from their superiors and coworkers. However, their approval-seeking behavior may cause them to become anxious because they are afraid that other people will not give them what they want or like them for who they are.

d. Fear of Embarrassment or Humiliation

In any context, anxious preoccupied individuals are worried about embarrassing themselves in front of others or being humiliated by others on an ongoing basis. From social settings to work environments, these individuals sometimes worry that they will say or do something that embarrasses them in front of others or that other people will laugh at them or make fun of them for no reason. The fear of being embarrassed can prevent anxious preoccupied individuals from speaking up and asserting their opinion, which can be detrimental to their professional growth and job performance. Furthermore, the fear of humiliation may cause anxious preoccupied individuals to try to hide the truth about themselves or even lie to avoid embarrassment.

For example...

You are attending a business dinner with some colleagues when you discover a document they have been working on is missing from the meeting room. You know that the completed document is in your briefcase, which is currently being carried out by one of your colleagues. You are afraid to tell them about the document because you know they will be embarrassed when they realize they have it in their possession. The meeting starts, and you internally debate whether or not you should tell them about the document later so everyone doesn't know that you have it. When the conversation moves to other topics, you are relieved that you didn't tell them. However, you become even more anxious because the document is still in your briefcase, and you are worried that someone will find out it was you who had the completed copy.

Anxious preoccupied individuals may get upset or feel remorseful about embarrassing themselves or other people in front of others if they don't say or do something. They also worry about whether people will be embarrassed by something they have done or said. These individuals may become so consumed with their own embarrassment that they fail to see what other people are thinking about them, which can prevent them from realizing their actions and words are not ruining their image in the eyes of others.

Many people with this attachment style worry and worry a lot about their identity and how other people perceive them in their professional lives. This can result in them having a lot of work-related anxiety because they are not sure that people like them as much as they think.

3. Difficulty Trusting Others at Work

Another way in which anxious preoccupied individuals present themselves professionally is by showing a lack of trust in their superiors or colleagues at work. Thus, they may continue to require more approvals for even the smallest of tasks or assignments rather than simply trusting that their colleagues will follow through on the agreed-upon plan. Their lack of trust can also make them nervous about whether others will complete projects on time, resulting in increased time spent on detailed planning and over-analysis.

What triggers this behavior?

a. Fear of Losing Control

Anxious preoccupied individuals tend to be overly worried about their ability to control the outcome of decisions and events in the workplace, which can result in a strong need for control over others' choices and outcomes. They may become upset when making decisions or assignments and spend a lot of time creating detailed plans without asking for assistance from their coworkers, as their fear of the unknown may lead them to decide against asking for help. This fear can also cause anxious preoccupied individuals to worry about what could happen if they don't take control of events and outcomes, leading them to push others away from decision-making processes.

For example...

You are on a project with one other person who is in charge of making the final decision. You and your coworker have been discussing the project's next steps for weeks, but you still need to decide what you will do next. You are upset because you haven't been able to come to a decision, and you are not sure what to do next. Your coworker is still determining what they will do next, too, but they feel like they should be in charge of making this decision. You often find yourself second-guessing what your colleague says, and you question their judgment, which makes you feel upset and frustrated with them. You want to make the final decision, but you don't feel like you can ask for their help to make that decision because that would mean letting go of control of the outcome.

When anxious preoccupied individuals fear losing control over events and outcomes, it usually means they must maintain control over others' actions to ensure the best outcome possible. They often won't ask for help or support because they fear letting go of the outcome. They may also become frustrated with others when they insist on making decisions, even when their input is not needed.

b. Need for Validation

Anxious preoccupied individuals tend to seek approval and validation from others about what they do and how others view them in both their professional and personal lives. Therefore, these individuals constantly seek reassurance and approval from others about their work performance or decisions that have already been made. Due to this need for validation, these individuals' trust in their superiors or colleagues at work may be limited, as they may spend a lot of time seeking approval before moving on to the next task or stepping out of their role to ask for help.

For example...

You and your manager are collaborating on a project. Although you were last in this situation some time ago, you want to ensure that you follow all the necessary steps. However, your manager has yet to ask you for any updates about the project, and it has been several days since the latest version was sent to your boss. You are starting to feel anxious, and you need to ask your manager if they have received the latest updates. However, you don't want to appear unprofessional and distracted if your manager has not received it yet. You wait a little longer and then ask your manager if they have gotten the latest updates, which makes you nervous and anxious. Your manager tells you they have received the updates and that they appear fine, but you are still nervous and anxious because you haven't heard back from your boss yet. You wait a little longer and then ask your manager again if they have received the latest updates around an hour after the first time. You feel pressured to ask three more times before finally speaking with your boss about the next steps for this project.

This habit can put the person in a position where they cannot express their thought process or feelings, making it difficult to communicate effectively with others. They may also make decisions and assignments for others without asking for their input, which can make them feel like they are not taking responsibility for the outcome of a project or assignment.

c. Perfectionism and Achievement

Anxious preoccupied individuals tend to be more of a perfectionist in their work performance and professional roles than other personality types. They typically want to make sure that they can present themselves in the best possible light at all times, which can make it difficult for them to trust others with certain tasks or assignments. They may also be prone to being overly critical of themselves and their performances.

For example...

You are working on a project with your team members and want it to turn out perfectly. While you have sent drafts of the project back and forth with your teammates, you still feel like more work needs to be done before your project is complete. You continue working on the report at home and researching on your own time to ensure you have everything you need. When your team members ask for the report, you tell them it will be finished soon, but you still need to finish working on it. You are starting to get tired of working on this project, and you are starting to feel like your teammates should be able to complete this project on their own. While they have some experience with these projects, they need to learn more about what is needed for this project at all times.

This will prevent anxious preoccupied individuals from stepping out of their roles to communicate effectively with other colleagues and decision-makers. They may feel like they are unable to step out of their role due to their perfectionistic tendencies, which can prevent them from delegating important tasks and assignments that need to be completed.

d. Impatience, Impulsiveness, and Irresponsibility

Anxious preoccupied individuals tend to be impatient and impulsive in decision-making. This can limit the effectiveness of their decision-making and make them unable to react promptly to what is occurring around them. Trusting others and delegating responsibilities can be difficult for anxious preoccupied individuals due to this impatience, impulsiveness, and irresponsibility.

For example...

This can happen in situations where you have your team members complete tasks and assignments. You may want to get the best people possible, but you always seem unhappy with those assigned to these tasks. You may change the person you delegate each task to, depending on their speed or how they carry themself while completing the task. However, if they do not meet your expectations and standards, you will go back to delegating tasks on your own instead of communicating with others about what is happening.

This can make it difficult for individuals to work with you or be a part of the team you lead. You will find yourself constantly being frustrated with others for not doing things in the way that you would prefer or having them complete tasks in a timely manner.

When anxious preoccupied individuals are faced with a decision, they often do not feel they have enough information available to make a decision. Therefore, they feel like they must continue searching for more information before deciding. This can lead to confusion and feelings of frustration in work situations, as they may need help to reach out to others with questions or concerns.

This behavior is often driven by their primary fears of failure and rejection, which cause them to resist change and risks. They want to avoid situations where they might be rejected or criticized and fear that someone else will make the wrong choice, which could lead to negative outcomes. Because they think it will help them avoid some of their biggest fears, their desire to control the outcome makes them feel more secure about their actions. However, it can also prevent others from working efficiently because anxious preoccupied individuals insist on being heavily involved in every step of a decision-making process and may stall or reject certain ideas and suggestions before even learning about the potential long-term impact of those decisions.

4. Inability to Deal With Conflict

Anxious preoccupied individuals often present themselves professionally by having trouble resolving disputes that arise in the workplace. They may attempt to avoid conflict altogether by seeking "help" from a third party. However, this approach may be unsuccessful because they are unable to articulate their problem or solution accurately, and the third party may end up blaming them for the dispute instead of finding a solution.

What triggers this behavior?

a. Afraid of Being Judged Negatively

This is an especially prevalent issue among those who work in close proximity to their colleagues, as they may be afraid of being judged negatively if the conflict is resolved poorly or severely. They do not want to "look bad" and may take the easy way out by simply avoiding the topic altogether with their colleagues, resulting in their inability to work effectively with their colleagues or present themselves in the best light possible.

For example...

Situations like this can happen where you have issues that need to be resolved or discussed with your colleagues. However, you may be afraid of voicing your opinions for fear that you will look bad to others or that someone else may not see things the way you do. Because of this, you will start avoiding these issues until they cannot be avoided any longer. You may avoid confronting others about an issue and instead vent to your coworkers about how much it bothers you or how annoying the person is that you are having the issue with.

This behavior can negatively affect your work relationships and make it more difficult to resolve issues that need to be addressed in a timely manner. This may cause others to view you as unreliable and unable to move past issues or confront people without using a third party.

b. Afraid of Confrontation

Anxious preoccupied individuals are often afraid of confrontation in the workplace and tend to avoid these types of situations by avoiding the topic altogether. They may also try to confront others quietly on their own, where they may misinterpret what they are saying or make damaging decisions out of anger. This can lead to failure and embarrassment in the workplace, especially if it is noticed by those in charge of the team or who have more power than you.

For example...

You have a particular issue or topic that needs to be resolved, but you are afraid of confronting others about it. Therefore, you will avoid bringing it up with your coworkers and wait until there is a time and place when you can safely bring it up with them. You are afraid they will not quite understand what you are saying and react negatively. This may cause you to feel frustrated with their inability to understand what you are saying and how hard it is for you to work with them.

Therefore, you will often try to get around this by talking to someone else about what is happening, who may try to speak on your behalf or make them aware of the issue. However, this might backfire because they may say intended or misinterpreted things, as they need to try to get your point across fully.

In situations like this, you may misjudge how other people will react to certain things or issues, making you feel frustrated and let down. Not only will you believe that things will not be resolved promptly, but you may also feel responsible for the problems or become unable to comprehend what others are saying or why they are saying it.

c. Fear of Negative Outcomes

Anxious preoccupied individuals fear that "fixing" a situation or problem will only lead to more issues or problems in the long run. This can cause them to avoid conflict altogether, as they cannot clearly articulate their views and objections to others. They may also avoid confrontation because they fear admitting mistakes will damage their reputation and work relationships. Their inability to effectively resolve workplace disputes may also make them feel isolated and alone when dealing with these problems.

For example...

You may be given some assignments or projects to work on. However, you might be afraid of doing them because you think they are not the right fit for your skillset or will be too hard to complete on your own. While this could be considered a good thing, it may mean that you are also thinking about your long-term career and what situations will help you grow and improve. However, if this becomes an issue where you are afraid of working on assignments or taking on projects because of these reasons, it can make it difficult for others to trust and believe in you as an employee or team member. This can lead to additional conflicts at work and other problems that arise.

In this situation, you must learn to work around the issue and push yourself to do a good job. This is so your actions will speak louder than your words, and people will see you can work on these assignments.

This can also improve your chances of getting more opportunities like these in the future, which is a great way to boost self-confidence and develop new skills.

d. Lack of Confidence

Anxious preoccupied individuals suffer from low self-esteem and low confidence when dealing with conflicts at work. They may feel they need to be more competent to take on a task or confront others about an issue that has arisen. This can often lead to them feeling inept and incapable of working with their colleagues, as they believe that others are better than they are at handling these types of things.

For example...

This can happen when you are at work with someone else and feel frustrated or annoyed by them. You might end up trying to "fix" things in your own mind so that you feel better about your work situation. For example, you might start doubting whether they even have the skillset required to deal with the issue at hand. You may also try to become manipulative and act like you understand the issue better than they actually do so that you can improve your relationship with them. This can often make it seem as though others are more capable of handling situations than you are and can cause them to view you as a poor employee or team member who is always causing problems.

In situations like this, you may also be tempted to try and talk behind someone's back or contact other people at work and discuss the issue with them, as they may not even realize that you have attempted to contact them, either in person or via email or phone. This is because they will not know what you have said (or things said behind their backs) and do not know how it could have ended up being misconstrued as a direct attack against them. This can make people anxious about these situations and bring more negative attention to the person dealing with the issue.

This behavior is the result of a combination of factors. One is a person's upbringing; each person has a different level of conflict tolerance, and this tolerance can be influenced by outside forces such as the values they absorb from others or just their upbringing as a whole (e.g., they may have been taught at home not to confront others). A second factor is personality; it varies among individuals and biological predispositions, such as how aggressive or passive a person might be. People with anxious preoccupied attachment are more prone to experience conflict when working with others because stress makes it difficult for them to think clearly and cope in changing situations.

These behaviors are common among people with anxious preoccupied attachment styles. However, you can learn how to manage these behaviors to develop more constructive and successful ways of interacting with others on your team or at work.

CHAPTER 8

WORKPLACE SUPERPOWERS OF ANXIOUS PREOCCUPIED ATTACHMENT

Despite the difficulties that an anxious preoccupied attachment style can cause in the workplace, there are certainly positive aspects that can help people excel at work. These "superpowers" can prove to be especially useful in situations where several people are involved in the work.

The following are some of the workplace superpowers of anxious preoccupied attachment style:

1. Likely to Detect and Alert Others to Workplace Problems

Individuals with anxious preoccupied attachment styles are often able to detect and alert others to the fact that something might be wrong at work. They are perceptive and intuitive, allowing them to pick up on the less obvious problems in their environment. Their ability to sense danger is what often causes them to become overly anxious and wary of any potential problems in their life. They know when something does not feel right, even if they might only sometimes be able to tell exactly why it does not feel right.

How do they show this behavior

a. Notice everything

When individuals with anxious preoccupied attachment styles begin working at a place, it is common for them to notice everything about their workplace. They will be able to sense if there are any problems in the place they work and will believe they need to speak up about these problems. This is due to their intuition and ability to pick up on things that other individuals might not have noticed. This can help them become someone who keeps the workplace safe, but it could also annoy their coworkers.

For example...

This scenario might occur at work where you have a number of personal development goals that you need to work on. You are aware of these issues, believe them to be important, and will often want to speak about them even if they are not that serious.

You may get frustrated if your coworkers do not agree with the things you are bringing up and act as if they won't take you seriously. You will feel like they do not understand just how serious of an issue this could be, so you will continue to try to convince them until they are able to realize the problem at hand. This can make it much more difficult for you to work with them because they may not always want to speak about issues that aren't a big deal.

You will also want to be sure that your coworkers are treating each other with respect and kindness, which can often cause conflict among your coworkers because of how sensitive you can be. You will be easy to get along with, but you can also get upset when things aren't going the way you need them to go.

While you may be able to detect the problems going on in your workplace, you should also be sure you are giving yourself enough time to evaluate the situation. It would help if you were careful not to assume that something is a problem without being able to produce any evidence that it is. You will want to avoid jumping to conclusions because it could cause you and others around you to work at cross purposes, which may make the situation even worse than it was before.

b. Be overly concerned about the place they work at

Because their attachment style causes them to be so anxious, individuals with anxious preoccupied attachment styles might become incredibly concerned about potential problems in their workplace. These issues could be as small as an unintentional mistake or as big as a dangerous situation. This can allow them to focus on more than just the project they are working on and help them to become a more detailed individual who is concerned with any potential problems in their workplace. However, it can also cause them to need help focusing on their work and ensuring they get to everything they need to be done.

For example...

A situation at work may cause you to become so concerned about the place you work that you start to notice problems that other people don't have any issues with. You may become irritated with your coworkers for not being as focused on workplace issues if you believe these problems are more significant than things that others can easily overcome. You could also try to persuade your coworkers to take notice of the problems and do something about them.

You do not always want to become so worried about this situation, however, because it can make you overly emotional and cause you to panic even if there is no reason to. You could also start seeing every little thing in a negative light and be overly negative toward yourself and your coworkers. This may make you resent your coworkers, which is detrimental in any situation where your team needs to work as a unit to complete a task.

While you may begin to overreact to problems in your workplace, you should be sure you are not exaggerating these issues. You should avoid making snap decisions about a situation simply because you believe action is required. You need to evaluate the situation instead of just having a knee-jerk reaction, which can cause you and your coworkers a lot of problems throughout your day-to-day life at work.

c. Get scared and think of the worst

Because individuals with anxious preoccupied attachment styles are constantly thinking of the worst possible thing that could happen in their workplace, it is common for them to get scared and imagine these things. This causes them to take extra precautions to make sure these problems never become a reality. However, this extra precaution can often cause errors in their work because they are so focused on preventing any negative outcomes that they might miss out on other ideas or solutions.

For example...

You're working on a project that has a deadline, but you're starting to worry it might take longer than expected to finish. You become worried about this because you believe that if no one does anything about it, there will be no way for the company to finish the project on time. You discover a mistake someone else made in your work and begin to worry about what might occur if this mistake is not caught. You then start putting your personal feelings toward the employees who worked on this project before you and start to believe that there was a reason they did not catch this error. While trying to fix this problem, you don't notice a different mistake in the work you have done, which could lead to further issues in the future.

You may also begin to feel like people are working against each other on your team and that no one trusts each other. This can cause a great deal of tension among your coworkers and make it harder for them to communicate while attempting to complete tasks as a team.

You must also ensure you are not preoccupied with the worst-case scenario, as this could cause you to lose your temper and become irate with those around you. If other options can solve the problem in your workplace, you must make sure you step back from the situation before reacting.

This superpower is used to try to fix potential problems in the workplace. While you may feel like something needs to be done about a problem, you will often miss out on other solutions because you are so focused on the issues that have occurred in your workplace. This can cause you and your coworkers to become frustrated with one another and may decrease work productivity.

It is important to remember that you do not always have to think of the worst possible scenario at work. You can ignore the issues that have arisen and continue focusing on the work you need to do for your team to get things done as a group.

2. Consistently High Work Performance

Another one of the workplace superpowers that come from having an anxious preoccupied attachment style is that you will be consistent in your work performance. You will always be consistent in your work ethic and try to remain that way. But it can also cause you to become single-minded and not take the time to know other people in your workplace.

How do they show this behavior

a. Self-Awareness and Structure

People with anxious preoccupied attachment styles are very self-aware and know what it takes to get things done in their lives. They may be able to achieve their personal objectives as a result of this. They will also be very aware of the emotions of people around them, which can help them to figure out how they can help them get things done. They can figure out the right structure for their workplace to make sure they can get things done and become a more productive member of the organization. But they may need to be more focused on accomplishing tasks instead of getting to know the people in their workplace, which can make them aloof and ignore people in their workplace.

For example...

You are collaborating with several people to complete a project you are working on that has a tight deadline. You try to figure out the best plan of action to meet this deadline and set the right structure for your workplace to accomplish this. Because they will have less time to work on other projects, the people you are collaborating with are displeased with the new structure you have established. While you may try to figure out what is bothering them, you may decide it is best to ignore their attitude and continue focusing on the structure of your workplace—resulting in you not taking the time to understand their needs or your own.

This situation can also be seen when you start ignoring the needs of your coworkers in your workplace. You might decide that you need more time to understand other people and their feelings in the workplace. This will result in their displeasure and may make it more difficult for you to communicate with others.

While you may be extremely good at getting things done, you need to be sure you take the time to know other people in your workplace and know how you can help them get things done. As long as you are consistent in your work, you can accomplish many tasks and become one of the most productive people on your team. But if you ignore other people's needs or only focus on accomplishing tasks, you will lose credibility with your coworkers.

b. Focused

People with anxious preoccupied attachment styles will be very focused on their work and how they can get things done. They are not easily distracted by the outside world and know how to focus on the task at hand. This can assist them in being highly productive members of their workplace and in completing their tasks in a timely manner. But they can also become obsessed with their work and forget to take a break from everything. This can make them very tired and stressed out by the time they get home from work.

For example...

While working on a project, you believe it is very important to get things done correctly. You take your time to determine the most efficient way to complete the project. While you may feel like it is taking longer than expected, you will remain focused on accomplishing the task at hand. You complete it and feel a sense of pride that you can accomplish all the tasks assigned to you. But the job remains unfinished by the time you get home from work, resulting in you having to work on the project all night so you can get it finished and turned in.

This situation can also be seen in people who only focus on accomplishing tasks that are most important to them. They might work on things that are less important to the organization and miss out on other tasks that could be completed more quickly. This will cause other people to become frustrated with them and may decrease work performance.

While it is essential to be able to focus on the tasks at hand and perform an outstanding job, you must also take breaks when necessary and allow yourself time to recover from workplace stress. For your workplace relationships to continue to run smoothly, it will be beneficial if you also ensure you are completing tasks that are vital to the organization and fulfilling your other responsibilities.

c. Highly Responsible

People with anxious preoccupied attachment styles can be highly responsible and take their job very seriously. Because they can figure out the best way to complete tasks and ensure they get things done on time, they will be a very reliable person in the workplace. They like to ensure they do a good job and remain highly responsible even if others need to take responsibility for their work. This can cause them to become frustrated when people around them are not completing tasks assigned to them or making sure that things get done properly.

For example...

As you begin a new project or assignment that requires you to gather a lot of information and complete tasks within a set amount of time. You work very hard to accomplish this task and ensure you are giving the best quality work possible. But one of your coworkers needs to complete their tasks more professionally, which can cause you to become frustrated and upset with them. You feel like they are not taking responsibility for their part of the job, which makes it difficult for you to feel comfortable in your workplace.

You will do whatever it takes to ensure that everything remains on schedule and gets finished correctly, even if it means that you have to take on more tasks to ensure that things are done correctly and that you will have everything done on time. This can cause you to become overworked, which could make you feel overwhelmed and stressed when you get home from work.

This situation can also be seen by people who place the blame for something going wrong in their workplace on other people. They may believe it is the other person's fault for not doing their part in getting tasks done, which causes them to become overwhelmed with trying to complete everything themselves.

Realize that everyone has different needs and can work in different ways. But it is important to know your needs and those of others in your workplace. You must learn how to collaborate with people who operate in different ways from you if you hope to manage your professional relationships successfully. This can help you accomplish tasks and help the organization function more efficiently.

This superpower can improve your performance at work and help you accomplish everything that needs to be done. But it is important to use this superpower cautiously and ensure you have others who can help get the most out of you. Taking good care of yourself will make it easier for the people around you to get things done.

This might change how people perceive you at work or treat you as a coworker. This may cause other coworkers not to trust or respect your opinions on what needs to be done or how tasks should be completed. Remember that everyone is different and has various needs and preferences when it comes to working together on a project.

3. Excellent Team Players

One with an anxious preoccupied attachment style can also be an excellent team player in the workplace. They can be hypervigilant with their actions and how they might be upsetting to others. As a result, they are unlikely to be workplace troublemakers; rather, they are likely to constantly evaluate their behavior and work quality to avoid conflict with other employees.

How do they show this behavior

a. Being Vigilant

Anxious preoccupied people are very attentive to their surroundings at all times. They will always be watching for any signs of possible conflict or discontent among coworkers, which can help them retain good employee relations and a positive work environment; their constant vigilance regarding their actions and words while at work may lead to them becoming overworked. They are constantly holding back when they should be letting go and relaxing to allow themselves to focus on completing tasks in the workplace.

For example...

You are very sensitive to how you are acting in the workplace, and you constantly need to reassure yourself that you are not being offensive or bothering other people around you. You want everyone to get along and do their part for the workplace to run smoothly. Because of this, you are afraid of doing something wrong or saying something that could offend someone. As a result, it is hard for you to relax while at work, making it difficult to focus on completing tasks.

This can cause you to become overworked and overwhelmed while trying to be professional when you are at work. And even though you'll probably do your best to maintain composure, this will probably make it difficult for you to carry out your duties effectively, which could make people think you don't know what you're doing or that your input is useless, which might make them disrespect your opinion.

While it is important to ensure that you are working in a positive environment, you should also be careful not to be too vigilant. Examine your thoughts and emotions to determine if you truly care about what others have to say or if you are attempting to avoid making a mistake. This way, you will give more input and help people understand your ideas when you have a good reason to make a certain suggestion.

b. Over-caring

Anxious preoccupied people can be over-caring as well. This could be observed in their work behaviors, where they attempt to be overly helpful and friendly with other coworkers, overburdening them with all the assistance they have provided to others throughout the day and all the tasks that need to be completed. This is likely because they feel like their coworkers may not understand or appreciate everything they do for them.

For example...

You are very sincere in helping your coworkers at work and want everyone to see that you care about their success. So much so that it is hard for you to say no when you are asked for help in anything you can do. You want everyone to feel comfortable and do a good job with whatever task you are given, making it difficult for you to prioritize what must be completed first. This could cause people around you to either feel overwhelmed by your helpfulness or not want the help in the first place because they may feel like it is a distraction from everything else they have going on at work that they need to focus on.

This situation may cause you to feel overwhelmed and like you are trying to do too much about the tasks assigned to you by those around you. You may become even more anxious because you are uncertain how people will respond to your work and how helpful you will be in completing it. But when you recognize this is what is happening, it can be helpful for you to find ways of coping with the situation before it gets out of hand.

While it is important to be helpful, it can also be good to focus on getting the work done that you need to complete. And at the same time, remember your coworkers also have their own tasks they need to complete, as well as their own lives and responsibilities outside of work. You should try your best to ensure you are not becoming over-emotional or over-sensitive because people may feel you need more respect for them or their needs if you are always offering too much assistance.

c. Good With Conflict

Anxious preoccupied people are often very good at handling conflict, even in the workplace. Because they become so focused on not upsetting anyone else, they are very good at working through disagreements between coworkers. They feel comfortable confronting others and discussing how things can be done differently if necessary. This can create a good work environment and a better understanding among coworkers. Still, they will often be overworked because they constantly have to deal with conflict in the workplace.

For example...

You are very good at settling other people's arguments and helping them understand each other's points of view. You are always trying to ensure everyone is getting along and know you have a responsibility to help resolve problems among coworkers. Therefore, it can be difficult for you to concentrate on completing tasks at work because you are constantly concerned with ensuring that everyone cooperates well. This can lead other coworkers to feel they cannot depend on you for help or support when they need it because you are constantly distracted by conflict at work.

This situation can also cause you to feel like you are putting too much effort into caring for other people when they are having trouble at work. This feeling can make it difficult for you to maintain a healthy work environment and prevent the workplace from deteriorating. It can even cause people who are more sensitive or emotionally invested in the workplace to feel they cannot depend on you for help, ultimately making them question your leadership skills.

While it is essential that you are a great team player, you should also pay close attention to your own needs. Be mindful of your thoughts and feelings, and try to understand how much time and energy you put into resolving conflict with coworkers. It would help if you tried to find ways to work through conflict that do not cause you to neglect other things that need your attention, such as completing tasks in the workplace. You can do this by reminding yourself of your strengths and setting limits on how much time and effort you spend on resolving conflict at work.

Being a good team player in the workplace is a desirable trait, but it requires dedication. Trust is the foundation of teamwork, and anxious preoccupied individuals may find it difficult to let go of their anxiety to trust those around them. This is why you need to be aware of your tendencies to become too emotional and overly sensitive, as well as how your anxious preoccupied temperament can affect your ability to function optimally in the workplace. When you take the time to recognize this and learn how to improve these tendencies, you will be able to increase your awareness of yourself and bring more balance into your life.

With these thoughts in mind, it is important to realize your strengths and how they can help you succeed at work. We all have different talents and abilities, but not everyone has a natural gift for every skill or task. But as long as you can find a way to use your strengths for the benefit of others, you can become a highly productive member of the workforce.

PART 3

OVERCOMING ANXIOUS PREOCCUPIED ATTACHMENT

CHAPTER 9

UNDERSTANDING MY TRIGGERS

If you find yourself frequently acting in a way you don't like, it may be best to consider why this is happening. If your actions are being driven by the needs of others rather than your own needs, then it might be time to confront those who trigger these responses from you. Sometimes other people are not even aware they are triggering strong emotional responses from you, and often, these responses can be very much out of proportion with the situation or even with the individual.

TECHNIQUES TO KNOWING WHAT TRIGGERS YOU

There are a lot of techniques that can help you to become more aware of how and why you respond in certain ways, like:

1. Imagery

Imagery is a technique in which you visualize your negative feelings and emotions. This helps you think about what you are feeling and precisely how you feel. It's a great way to see the problem from another perspective, change how you view situations, and learn how to problem-solve in stressful or emotional situations. During a panic or anxiety attack, it can be difficult to comprehend what is wrong with you or why you feel so overwhelmed. Imagery can help you make sense of things and show you that feeling overwhelmed is okay.

How to do this?

Step 1: Create an image of what you are feeling.

Start by taking a deep breath and relaxing your body. You can do this by simply closing your eyes or taking deep breaths. Put yourself in a calm and relaxed state by thinking about something that has nothing to do with the current situation or anything that could lead to anxiety.

Step 2: Describe the feelings that you're having.

Once you've started breathing calmly and deeply, take a minute to describe in detail what you are feeling about what's happening at the moment. Describe what you're thinking and feeling and why you feel this way.

Answer the following questions:

- How do you feel about what's happening?
- How do you feel about this person/situation?
- What are all the reasons that you are feeling this way?
- What beliefs do you have that make you feel this way?

- What do you want to happen at this moment?

The more detailed you can answer, the more effective this technique will be.

Step 3: Give the feelings a name, like anxiety or stress.

Now that you have described what you are feeling, decide on a name for these feelings. If there is some reason you feel stressed, anxious, or angry at times, try to think of something else to call it. You could call it "anxiety" or just "stress." If someone else made you angry or stressed, then maybe think about another word for this feeling, such as "upset," "irritated," or even "annoyed."

Once you've decided on the word, write it down. Write it down so you can remember this feeling the next time you feel anxious.

Step 4: Decide where you feel them in your body.

Take a few deep breaths again, relax your body, and take a minute to decide where you feel these feelings in your body. Even though emotions can be intense, we often don't know where they are coming from. By pinpointing the exact feelings you are experiencing in your body, thinking about how those feelings are manifesting and working with them will become easier. Note with as much specificity as possible how these emotions affect your body.

Try answering these questions:

- Does it hurt somewhere?

- Do you feel a lump in your throat?

- Perhaps your cheeks are flushed, or certain muscles are tense?
- Does your chest feel tight or full?
- Are there any sensations in your stomach?
- Does your back hurt?
- Does it feel like you can't catch your breath?

By knowing what physical symptoms accompany negative feelings, you can learn to recognize them when they come up, making it easier for you to work through them. If you are nervous about doing this exercise, make it as simple as possible and start with something minor, like tension in your back.

Step 5: Repeat the process if necessary.

Take several deep breaths and loosen up your muscles. Then take a few more deep breaths and concentrate again on how you feel about the situation. If necessary, repeat the previous steps until you have regained a calm state of mind.

This technique is best used when feeling anxious, worried, or panicked. You can use it when you feel like something is wrong and don't know what it is or what it will be like. You can also use this technique when nothing is particularly wrong, but anxiety still invades your mind. Imagery is an excellent way to explore how you feel without risking any harmful real-world incidents.

2. Journaling

Journaling is an excellent method for gaining emotional insight. It is a method for examining your life and identifying the causes of your emotions. It is an excellent way to learn more about your mind's inner workings and how it reacts to the outside world. The actual process of journaling is quite simple but requires a certain amount of time to master.

How to do this?

Step 1: Get a journal.

The first step is to get yourself a journal. It can be any size, but it should fit comfortably in your lap, and you should be able to use it easily. You can find journals in the bookstore, a local department store, or even an office supply store. You can make your own journal by using loose-leaf paper or regular notebook paper, but for the best results, you will want to buy something specifically designed for journaling.

Step 2: Sit down somewhere private and quiet

It will help if you had some private time where you will not be disturbed. This may be in a library or even at work, but it needs to be a place that is free of distractions and completely quiet. It will help if you also go somewhere where you don't mind the smells of other people.

Step 3: Write freely.

You can write everything down that comes to your head—it can be descriptions of a scene from your life, concepts about life in general, or just random thoughts that may come from nowhere. It will help if you write down whatever is on your mind. You can start by writing a few words and then building on them as you go. For example, you write the word "anxious" and try to expand upon that; you can write more words like "worried" and "anxious" and add more details.

Step 4: Learn from the entries.

After you have written in your journal, don't just toss it aside. Look over your entries and identify trends. If some days you feel excited about life and other days you feel angry, then try to identify why this happens. Maybe things happen at work that make you feel positive on some days and negative on others—don't ignore this! If a pattern emerges, write down the typical situations that set off your emotions and how you can avoid or deal with them in the future. If you do this right, you can learn a lot about yourself.

Step 5: Remember your emotions.

You can use this journaling technique to help you remember how you feel. Reflect on your entries and remember the emotions they provoke. Try to experience all of your emotions and gain as much knowledge as possible about them. This will help you better understand your emotional life and keep you from being overwhelmed by your feelings.

Journaling is an excellent method for bringing one's concerns into the open, where they can be addressed. It is a special kind of therapy that can be done alone, but it still helps to deal with your emotions. It is also a great way to remember how you feel and how you can deal with those feelings.

3. Talking to someone

Communicating with others is a straightforward and effective method for understanding and connecting with your emotions. A friend, your partner, or even your family can all be great people to talk to about your feelings. Talk to someone who is great at spending time with you but also listens attentively and doesn't interrupt or judge your feelings. Someone who is empathetic and understanding is crucial. The more they know about how you feel, the more they will understand what it's like for you, how it feels, why it happens, and what goes along with these feelings. Talking to someone like this will encourage their listening skills, and because they care about your feelings, they may actually listen carefully to understand them better.

Talking to someone is different from just sharing your feelings, though, because when you talk to someone, you are actually trying to make a difference. You are trying to get them to understand how you feel so that you won't get the same response when you bring up these feelings again. Talking with others can help you realize why things feel so wrong. Don't just accept things because they are there—learn to recognize what is causing your emotional problems and then work to solve them. If the person you're talking to doesn't understand what you're saying, don't let that stop you from talking; this may be the opportunity you need to find someone who can listen and help inspire new ideas for how to deal with these problems.

4. Talk to a professional

Some of the triggers may be hidden, so uncovering them may require help from a trained healthcare professional. There are lots of psychiatrists and psychologists out there who specialize in emotion-related issues. They will be able to assist you in attaining a state of calm over the phone or in-person.

Things to consider when choosing a psychologist

a. Your belief system

To undertake therapy with a psychologist, it is important that you feel comfortable talking about certain things with them. Therapy is not always effective, and some individuals may find it difficult to discuss certain experiences and emotions in the presence of a therapist. On the other hand, the therapist must have a similar background to you so they can fully understand your experiences.

b. Issues that may arise

It will help if you also think about whether you can talk to the psychotherapist without feeling upset. Finding a therapist who is flexible and responsive to problems as they appear is crucial. If things get difficult, it is good to know that the therapist will have a way of dealing with situations so you stay relaxed and are not worried about discussing things in detail. A good therapist should also be able to obtain information without invading your privacy, which means you feel safe talking openly about these issues with them.

c. Location

You also need to consider the difficulty in traveling to your chosen therapist, as any distance will make it difficult for a regular conversation. If you can travel, this can be an advantage as it enables you to meet the psychotherapist face-to-face so there can be a more personal connection and comfort as well. However, if traveling is out of the question, then find out their working hours so your calls can be scheduled within them.

d. Fees

You must know the fees before going ahead with therapy sessions so you are not shocked by a bill at the end. Make sure you find any additional fees that might arise, such as if you wish to continue with the therapist after a certain period. These additional fees can be very helpful in staying within your budget, but it is always good to know what the upfront costs are so you are not surprised by a big bill at the end.

e. Guarantee

Finding out if there are any guarantees is crucial when looking for a therapist. This means that if your personal issues start to get worse at some point in therapy, then you will be able to seek help from that particular psychotherapist again. Insurance companies often guarantee therapists for a certain period of time after your first session, which may help you decide whether or not the therapist is right for you.

Talking to someone outside of you and your close friends will allow you to expose your hidden feelings without fear of judgment. They can also give you new perspectives on dealing with these feelings, inspire new ideas you haven't thought of before, and give support when you need it most.

Emotions are very easy to feel but often hard to understand. When you first start feeling emotional about certain things, getting along with the rest of the world can be difficult. These feelings can just come out of nowhere, and even if you try to ignore them, they still won't go away. Not only do these feelings cause tension in interactions with others, but they also create pressure within yourself. Therefore, it is important that you recognize what is causing these feelings so you can learn how to deal with them.

Emotions are a part of our daily lives, and we interact with other people without realizing just how painful our feelings can be. One of the main problems associated with emotions is that we must be taught about the different feelings we experience and why they occur. We begin to associate emotions with a specific situation or event, often without being able to give any reason for why those emotions are occurring. Given a chance, you will recognize all kinds of emotions in yourself and others. You will see a variety, including joy, sadness, and distrust or jealousy. Learn how to deal with your emotions to manage your life better and have a lower stress impact on everyone around you.

MANAGING YOUR TRIGGERS

Many techniques have been proven to help people keep their emotions under control. These techniques can be used in all types of situations, from dealing with difficult emotions to learning how to control anger and frustration. If you feel that your emotions could be getting the best of you, then it is important that you learn the techniques to stay on top of your feelings.

1. Exercise

Physical activity is one of the best methods for releasing negative emotions. Since exercise creates a great endorphin release, it can often alleviate many symptoms and make you feel better about yourself and the situation. It can help you manage your emotion by "getting your mind off it" and will often help you feel better after the fact.

Some Simple Exercise Ideas

a. Walking

Walking is a great way to release stress, and as a result, this can often cause you to feel better again. It is also easy to release your emotions, so if you are angry, walk it off. The best way to walk off your emotional outburst is by picking up your pace and getting into the right mood before starting. Getting into a slow and steady rhythm will allow you to think about other, more pleasant things that are going on around you, as well as reduce your emotional tension.

It is recommended that individuals walk for at least 30 minutes per day, as this provides numerous mental and physical advantages. During this time, you can focus on other positive things that are going on around you, and as a result, it will make you feel better in the end.

Additionally, walking at various times of the day can be beneficial. You are free to choose whenever is most convenient for you, but it is often best to schedule outdoor walks during the day when there are many other people around. This will provide more social stimulation and help you have more positive interactions with someone else, which can also help you manage your emotions better.

b. Going to the Gym

Going to the gym is another great way to keep your emotions under control. Not only will you be able to exercise, but you are also in a controlled environment with many people around that can support you in your journey. Using all the free weights and machines can provide you with a great workout and encourage positive social interactions with other gym members or trainers. This makes it easier for you to release all of your feelings so that you do not have to carry them around with you for so long.

It is important that the gym has the right equipment for exercising, which will often give patients a better overall experience. Taking part in small or large-group training sessions is just one of the many activities you can do while exercising. This can be done so you can coordinate with other members and and learn together how to properly manage emotions. Additionally, it can be a fantastic way to work with others on various physical and mental difficulties.

c. Sports

Playing sports is a great way to release both physical and mental tension. Sports are fun, and the opportunities for interaction are endless. If you are looking for more interaction with other people, then sports can work wonders for you. They will help you get involved in many different activities, which is the best way to manage your emotions!

It can also be beneficial to learn new sports that involve interacting with others. Sports involving teamwork often make it easier for you to get along better with others and motivate you to reach your goals faster. This will provide a lot of confidence or motivation when dealing with your emotions, no matter what they may be at any given time.

d. Gardening

Gardening can be a great way to manage your anger if you live in a place where it is possible. Gardening is a great way to interact with nature, allowing you to manage your anger in several ways. For example, planting flowers and vegetables can help you release emotions if they are coming from inside you. The fresh air and the fact that there are many other people around make it easier for you to manage your emotions by spending more time outside in nature.

Planting requires you to take care of the outside world, which may serve as a reminder of what needs to be done and provide motivation to ignore internal issues for a limited time. It allows you to spend more time outdoors and can be a great way of diverting your attention. This is also beneficial because it allows you to take responsibility for something else to keep yourself occupied.

2. Meditation

Learning to meditate is not that difficult, making it even better! If meditation can also help you manage your emotions, then it might be a great idea for you to learn how to do this. This will allow you to release all of your emotions at the same time.

Although it's not always simple to meditate, with more practice, it will get simpler. It is recommended that you start with simple meditation techniques that don't require much time or focus. These should be practiced as often as possible to improve your focus and mindfulness over time. These skills will help you better manage your emotions when you become overly emotional about something or someone.

How to do this?

Step 1: Find a Place

Find a quiet place where you will not be easily interrupted. You are free to sit on the floor or a chair as long as your back is straight and your legs are crossed.

Step 2: Find a Focus Point

Focus on breathing slowly and regularly. It will help if you try to breathe from your nose and fill up the air in your lungs before exhaling almost completely out of your mouth. It will help if you try to breathe at the same rate while meditating, which will keep you relaxed and prevent you from overexerting yourself and tiring out too fast. You can raise your arms above your head when you breathe to help you focus on the breath and get rid of some tension in your body.

Step 3: Become Present

Become present. Allow yourself to be here. Focus on what is happening right now rather than worrying about anything else in the past or future. It will be beneficial if you attempt to concentrate on what is occurring around you, whether it be the sounds of cars, birds, or people. Try to find as many things around you as possible.

Step 4: Breathe Regularly

Continue to breathe slowly and regularly and do so for about 3-5 minutes. Just focus on your breath. Each exhalation should take about three seconds, and each inhalation should also take about three seconds. If your mind wanders, bring your attention back to your breath. So you do not have to keep track of time while meditating, you can also use an alarm to signal when you are finished.

Step 5: Relaxation and More Focus

You can repeat steps 1-4 as often as you'd like. You may also perform the same action with your eyes open. Try looking around, focusing on something in front of you if possible, while meditating and allowing yourself to be present each time. This is a good way to manage your emotions. Stay relaxed and focused! If your mind wanders, bring your attention back to your breath.

Meditation is not something that you can do instantly. It takes time to master, so be patient and give it a shot! You'll eventually notice how your brain changes during meditation. You will see how your mind tends to wander, and you will realize that it isn't always because of outside circumstances or things that happened in the past. This skill will help you better manage your emotions when you become overly emotional about something or someone. You will begin to notice that you can focus on one thing, even the breath, and then your emotions will become easier to control.

3. Music

Music therapy may be a good way to manage your emotions. It has been shown to improve mood and help you relax. Music can affect both the body and mind, which is why it can help relieve stress and, as a result, help you manage your emotions better.

It might be a good idea to listen to particular types of music when you are emotionally out of control because music can have a much stronger impact than you might think. Music therapy is often helpful when you are trying to relax or de-stress. Listening to certain kinds of music that relieve stress can help you manage your emotions better than ever before. This can also make dealing with your emotions easier and more manageable. It is important that everyone finds the kind of music that works for them individually because everyone processes music in different ways.

Listening to music can also help you make better choices. For example, listening to upbeat music can make you feel better and get your mind off things when you are feeling emotional. If something is bothering you and the upbeat music can't distract you, then try listening to a slow song. Calm music might help you feel relaxed enough to think about things more clearly or even see the situation from a different perspective.

Some people may choose to listen to certain kinds of music during meditation and meditate at certain times of the day when it is calming outside or inside, for example. This helps them keep their emotions in check and learn how to manage them best in everyday life.

4. Breathing Techniques

Breathing techniques are one of the best ways to manage your emotions. They help you relax, feel more self-assured, and relieve stress. Breathing techniques can be very simple yet very effective at relieving stress and tension.

The following are some of the techniques you can use:

a. Breathe in and Out Deeply

This is one of the most basic breathing techniques. It is also known as the alternate nostril breathing technique and is very effective in controlling emotions. It uses the art of alternately breathing the right and the left nostrils, which helps balance and strengthen both sides of the brain and facilitates better brain functioning, thus reducing stress and anxiety. The right nostril is connected with the left brain, which is rational and logical, while the left nostril is connected with the right brain, which is emotional. Stimulating one or both nostrils stimulates both parts of your brain, leading to a more balanced state of mind.

How to do this?

Step 1: Sit up straight and relax your body.

Step 2: Place the thumb of the right hand just behind the left ear and place the two fingers of that hand up to the nose, just at the nostril.

Step 3: Now inhale deeply by breathing in through both nostrils alternately, slowly, and evenly. As you do this, stretch both arms straight and bend them slowly over your head until they touch each other. Keep your eyes closed while you do this.

Step 4: Now exhale completely through both nostrils while keeping your eyes closed. After you have exhaled completely through both nostrils, bend your arms to touch each other again in front of you before straightening them out again.

Step 5: Repeat this process for about 10-20 minutes.

These breathing techniques can be done as often as you like. Many people do it daily to relieve their stress, improve their mood, and so on. These breathing techniques are important to manage your emotions because they energize both sides of your brain and stimulate brain function.

b. Square Breathing

Square breathing is a common technique used for relaxation, high performance, or wellness. It involves using four different counts through both nostrils, starting from 1-4-1 (or 4-1-4) and finishing with only 1-4. Many people can do this very relaxing breathing while sitting on the couch, watching TV, or during meditation.

How to do it?

Step 1: Sit up straight and relax your body. Take slow deep breaths through both nostrils (preferably in the morning because we wake more relaxed).

Step 2: Place the first finger of your right hand between your eyebrows on the bridge of your nose. Place your second finger outside the right nostril.

Step 3: Now exhale quickly through the right nostril by counting out loud, "1," and inhale slowly through the left nostril by counting out loud, "4," while looking at the finger on your nose.

Step 4: Now breathe out from the left nostril in the same manner by counting out loud, "4," and inhale through the right nostril, counting out loud, "1."

Step 5: Close the left nostril with your thumb, breathe out from the right nostril in the same manner by counting out loud, "1," then inhale through the left nostril by counting out loud, "4." You have now finished one round of square breathing.

Step 6: Keep repeating this round 3 times.

Square breathing is supposed to help cool your brain, calm you, and relax you. Like alternate nostril breathing, it stimulates both sides of the brain and balances them.

c. Reverse breathing

This breathing technique helps to relax the mind as well as the body by using what is known as "diaphragmatic breathing." This helps increase oxygen intake into the system while also allowing more carbon dioxide (a waste product) to be released. Diaphragmatic breathing is done by taking a deep breath through both nostrils and then filling the lungs before exhaling almost completely out of your mouth.

How to do this?

Step 1: You can either lie on your back or sit with your feet flat on the ground and your arms at your sides in a chair.

Step 2: Inhale slowly through both nostrils, feeling the belly swell up with air. You should try to inhale completely without any gaps in between.

Step 3: After you have filled your lungs with oxygen, exhale slowly through both nostrils, only trying to squeeze out just enough air so the breath can be felt, leaving the body and not pushing out a lot of air at once. This helps to prevent energy loss and provides good exercise for the diaphragm muscle.

Step 4: Continue breathing like this for 15-30 minutes daily. Make sure you begin slowly so your body gets used to the breathing pattern gradually over time. There is no need to push yourself when using this technique; allow your body to breathe slowly and comfortably for 15-30 minutes daily.

This breathing technique is best done when free in nature or the trees. Taking deep breaths from the lower abdomen helps you relax, feel more alert, and focus on things around you.

Breathing techniques are used frequently as relaxation and stress management tools to achieve a more relaxed state of mind. Instead of acting on your emotions immediately, you should take a few deep breaths before letting them get the better of you.

By knowing how to manage your emotions, you can take better action on the issues that arise in your life to move forward successfully. Fall and get back up again; you'll be amazed at how much stronger you'll feel after doing so. If you are feeling depressed or feeling down, try a different approach. Realize that you possess the ability to alter your life. This is the time for positive changes in your life, and if you make them, they will change the course of your destiny.

CHAPTER 10

IMPROVING YOUR SELF-CONFIDENCE

As anxious preoccupied attachment can lower your self-confidence, it may help you see yourself in a more realistic light. This does not mean you should delude yourself and believe you are someone you are not, but having a realistic idea of your own abilities and strengths is really important when it comes to building your self-confidence. It's also crucial to watch out for inflated and unrealistic self-perceptions as well as self-doubt turning into your main source of negativity.

As confidence is built, it will begin to carry across all areas of your life, which can be a great start toward building a healthier relationship with yourself. Confidence will also help you move towards achieving success in your relationships and can give you that boost you need to improve the way you approach others so contact with those who are important to you can be more positive than before.

WAYS TO IMPROVE SELF-CONFIDENCE

1. Change Your Belief About Yourself

If your self-confidence needs to be better and you need more than just a boost, you should have a new belief about yourself. It's time to change the way you think about yourself and your abilities. It will help if you switch the negative thoughts and beliefs that tell you you're not as good as your friends or that you are better than them at certain things with some positives to feed your brain. The first step is to create a new belief about yourself.

There are various ways to accomplish this, including:

a. Learn to Accept Yourself

Accepting yourself is one of the most important things you can do to feel better about yourself. You must learn to accept yourself, first and foremost, as a person.

You will not be able to change anything about your current physical appearance, but you can change things that are more reflective of your inner self-worth. You may not be perfect, but learning to accept yourself will make your life more enjoyable and less stressful. Accepting yourself will also make you feel more confident and self-assured, which will come in handy for many of the other steps.

How to do this?

i. Focus on what makes you unique and proud of who you are now.

Some individuals have difficulty focusing on their positive qualities. Although they may focus on who they are and what they have accomplished, it is challenging to find anything admirable about themselves. If you are still looking for one thing you like about yourself, start off by focusing on something that is not necessarily physical. Think of something distinct about you personality-wise, such as your sense of humor or your way of handling certain situations that you've experienced in the past. Think about something about yourself that you're proud of, and when you think about it, be proud of yourself for doing so.

This will help you recognize your identity and appreciate what you are good at. That way, you can focus more on the positive aspects of yourself and not worry about all the things you don't like.

ii. Accept that everyone is different.

Everyone has their own personality and style. It is acceptable for individuals to be unique. The actions of the past do not define who you are currently. Everyone goes through a different set of struggles, and everybody has obstacles in their life. You have a choice in whom you spend your time and energy on and what you focus on.

Everyone has different roles in life. Some people will focus on getting the best grades possible, while others will focus on their careers. There will always be a few things you cannot change, but there are also many things you can do to improve your situation and make it easier for yourself to overcome them.

Everyone has some things they don't like, and it's okay to accept them. You may not be perfect, but you can still be a good person at the same time. Everyone makes mistakes, and that is completely normal.

No matter how much you change or try to avoid doing something that might reflect negatively on you, it will only help so much when something happens. When something does happen, people will go about it in different ways depending on their personality type. Still, people will continue to judge you on your character rather than who you are physically.

iii. Be kind to yourself.

No matter how much time passes, the past cannot change who you are or how you will feel about certain things in life. If you feel like you haven't done anything worthwhile with your life or feel like there is nothing special about who you are right now, remember that there is always something good to focus on or be happy about.

Being kind to yourself when you don't feel good can help you become a more positive person and give you the strength to achieve your dreams.

Being kind to yourself is all about thinking positively and having the self-confidence to improve on the things that will make your life better. Being positive and accepting that people will always have their opinions helps you not let what other people think to affect you as much. It will also help keep people's opinions of you from changing who you are as a person. All you can do is be happy with yourself and accept what you have done and what you will continue to do in the future.

iv. Learn to take care of yourself.

Your body is made to handle a lot of stress and negativity. Living a stressful and negative lifestyle can build up in your body and make you uncomfortable. When you feel uncomfortable, the body will signal to your brain what needs attention and healing. The more stressed your body is, the more signals it will send and the more pain it will have when something bad happens.

People often neglect their bodies which can lead to health problems later on in life. By neglecting your health, you put your body at risk for issues that can later prove to be more harmful than helpful. A healthy lifestyle involves eating well and exercising frequently, but it also involves learning the value of self-care by taking care of your body.

If you want to learn how to take care of yourself, keep doing what you're doing. Just make sure you take the time and space to learn how to better care of yourself.

v. Refuse to Be the Victim/Victimize Yourself.

If you have a history of self-victimization, it is time to break the pattern.

There is a difference between seeking revenge and seeking justice. If you're looking for revenge, it will affect your well-being and overall happiness. If you're looking for justice, then it's more likely that you'll get what you have been wanting.

What are some things that motivate people to seek revenge over justice? Well, when people seek revenge and don't get what they want, they will continue to seek it until they get what they want or give up altogether.

When people seek revenge, they usually victimize themselves by blaming themselves for the incident and feeling like they have been wronged. Imagine yourself in someone else's position and consider your feelings. If they committed an offense, would you be able to forgive them?

J.K. Rowling once said, "Happiness can be found even in the darkest of times if one only remembers to turn on the light." This goes hand and hand with many people using self-victimization because they can't see past their problems and are too reliant on their problems that they use it as an excuse not to take action. They think that if they don't act against themselves because of self-victimization, no one else will help them.

To break out of a cycle of self-victimization, it is essential to concentrate on the present rather than the past. You cannot change the past, but you can change how you perceive it and how it affects your life. It's understandable to have some resentment or anger towards certain people who might have hurt you in the past, but it's not okay to use that as an excuse for why things are going wrong in your life now.

Accepting oneself is the first step when it comes to self-confidence. It will be hard, considering your attachment type, but it will make you happy in the long run.

b. Positive Affirmations

Negative thoughts are part of the human condition, and many people find they have bad thoughts frequently. This is normal, and it's natural to feel down or upset sometimes. However, positive affirmations are not just for feeling down; they can be used whenever you need an extra boost, whether during your workday or in stressful moments in life.

Positive affirmations are a way of using positive self-talk to improve the quality of life. They work by focusing on improving certain aspects or traits you have or want to have. Each positive affirmation aims to instill a more positive thought in the mind while eradicating a negative one.

More than just self-affirmation, positive affirmations are also based on a concept called "anchoring." Anchoring is a cognitive process that involves using an association to form new learning and memory experiences. In this case, the new learning experience is how you want to think and feel about yourself. Positive affirmations tap into your subconscious mind and help you to remember how you want to feel by associating it with an already existing experience or memory. By repeating positive affirmations and using them to anchor yourself in a calm and confident state, you can improve your self-confidence.

How to do this?

Step 1: Identify the positive affirmation that relates to your goal.

For example:

"I am a confident person who always achieves my goals."

"I have a calmer, more composed state of mind."

"I am able to enjoy my hobbies and my life without distractions."

"I love myself."

"I feel great when I smile."

"Today is a great day."

"I am relaxed and calm."

"I feel confident when I use my intuition."

"I am free from stress."

"I love life and enjoy every moment."

"I am confident and happy."

"I am a healthy and beautiful person."

"I love myself because I am confident about so many things."

"I am confident when I interact with others."

These are just some examples of positive affirmations that may work for you, but select one that feels right and is relevant to your goal. You can also write your own affirmation. It is most effective when it comes from the heart and genuinely reflects your feelings about yourself or others.

Step 2: Repeat the affirmation to yourself.

Be sure to say it with feeling and emotion. Repeat it as often as possible, especially when you feel emotional or nervous. You can say it to yourself in the morning, throughout the day, or before going to sleep. The more you repeat it, the more you will anchor yourself and truly believe what you say.

Step 3: Be aware of how you feel when repeating positive affirmations.

Try and tune into your body and notice how different parts of your body react when listening to the affirmation. You may notice your breathing, heart rate, or blood pressure changing. These physical changes are a response to your inner feelings, which can help you recognize the state you are in when feeling confident and happy.

Step 4: Be aware of how you feel after repeating positive affirmations.

Pay attention to any emotional changes following the affirmation. If you notice any emotional change in yourself, it can be a great sign that the affirmation is working. Emotions such as happiness, joy, and excitement indicate that the affirmation positively affects how you feel inside.

Positive affirmations can also be used to achieve your life goals. They can help increase your self-confidence and change how you look at the world around you.

Changing your mindset is an essential method for enhancing your self-confidence and self-esteem. This may appear challenging, but it is not as challenging as you believe. It begins with learning to become conscious of one's own thoughts and then proceeding from there. You can then learn how to change your negative thoughts into more positive ones, which will ultimately make you feel more confident and positive about yourself. Your life and the lives of those around you will improve as a result.

2. Have a Clear Vision and Goal for Life.

Having a clear life vision and goal can help build self-confidence and increase motivation. By giving you the assurance and control you require to feel more in charge of your destiny, having a clear vision for the future will enable you to accomplish your goals with a greater sense of purpose.

How to do this?

a. Set Realistic Goals

You may wish to establish objectives for your career, relationships, or other aspects of your life. It can be helpful if these goals are realistic; sometimes, it may be better not to set unrealistic expectations, as this could lead to feelings of failure later on when those expectations aren't met. This can be particularly damaging if other people set these unrealistic expectations, or the expectations come from you subconsciously wanting to be liked or accepted.

Goals like, "I am going to get promoted at work," or "I am going to be an actress and star in a blockbuster movie," may seem unrealistic and even impossible to achieve, but instead, you could set more feasible goals such as, "I am going to study hard, my boss will notice my hard work, and I will get promoted." There are all sorts of ways this goal could be reached; such as, if you don't feel ready for a promotion, you can ask your boss if you can still do the job but with added responsibilities. Set goals that are realistic, as this can ensure that you don't feel like a failure later on in life.

b. Develop A Plan to Accomplish Your Goals

It is also important that you develop a plan for how you intend to achieve your goals and ambitions. Record what you must do, how long it will take, and when you anticipate completing the task (or tasks). You can also decide if you will achieve this goal (or goals) in one go or over a period of time. You could decide that you will try to achieve your goal (or goals) by starting off small, then gradually increase the intensity of your effort from there until you reach your desired goal (or goals).

You could also decide not to set a specific target for your goal (or goals) but instead commit to completing a task on a regular basis. When you have achieved this task, do another one and keep on repeating this until you have achieved your ultimate goals and have nothing left to accomplish. This way, you will continually push yourself to achieve your dreams, and it will be much easier for you to see where your strengths are and what areas you need to improve. You will also recognize if your original plan does not seem to be working or is filled with flaws, and you will then have time to come up with a new plan before continuing to push toward your ultimate goals and dreams.

It can be beneficial if you record your progress and achievements each day. For example: "I went for a walk this morning; I now have the strength to do other activities during the day. I also participated in class today, which was fun and helped boost my confidence." You could also make yourself a "to-do list" with two columns: one for tasks and one for checkmarks. This will help you track your progress and recognize where you are going wrong so that you have time to improve upon deficiencies in your plan or schedule.

c. Get External Support

It can be helpful to get external support when trying to achieve goals and dreams, such as getting friends or family members to help you set goals, structures, and plans for achieving those goals. You could also join a group of individuals who share your values and beliefs, as this will provide you with additional motivation and support to achieve your objectives. You could join an online forum or chat board for advice on how to complete tasks more efficiently or get extra guidance from other people who are either in the same situation as you or have completed similar tasks in the past. You could also gain inspiration and motivation from the experiences of others who have set comparable (or even more ambitious) goals than you.

You can also decide that you will not need to set goals yourself; instead, others will achieve your goals. For instance, if your objective is to gain weight, you could decide that weight loss is objective and then ask others via conversations or written correspondence what they believe you should do to achieve this objective. You could also ask them what they think would make a good diet plan for you, and they may suggest some books or websites to get more information on how to lose weight. When asking others for assistance, it is often best to offer to assist them in achieving their own objectives, as this will give you something to work toward and help you build relationships with others through mutual support.

d. Reward yourself for progress made and achievements

Expectation and motivation can be key factors in the achievement of goals, so it can be helpful to reward yourself for progress made and achievements to increase your motivation.

For example, you could decide that each time you achieve your task on a to-do list, you will give yourself a reward, such as buying yourself a new pair of shoes. You can also decide that each time you exercise at the gym, you will reward yourself with a little break from work or a round of mini golf at the local leisure center. This can be an especially helpful way of rewarding yourself, as rewarding yourself after completing tasks is easy. You don't want to set too many rewards, which can lead to unrealistic expectations and demotivation.

Your goals and ambitions are very important, as they can determine what you do with your life and how successful you are at achieving all your dreams, aspirations, and ambitions.

Your self-confidence will also be highly influenced by your goals, as this will determine how good you feel about yourself and what sort of things you can do in life.

3. Create A Well-balanced Life.

Another way to help you feel confident and happy about yourself is to create a well-balanced life. You can do this by remembering that the quality of your life is what matters, not just how busy or stressed you are all the time.

How to do this?

a. Spend time with your family and friends

You might feel better about yourself and your life if you spend time with your friends and family. It will also mean you have people to turn to for advice and support when needed.

Your friends and family are also good sources of motivation, as they will be able to encourage you and give you additional encouragement and support when you need it. They also help you stay motivated and on track with your plans, as they will usually understand what you are going through.

b. Make time for yourself

Retaining a healthy self-esteem level requires giving yourself the time you deserve. This is important so that when other people invite you to go out for dinner or see a film, you can say yes without feeling like you have to please others and take their offer because of an egocentric view about yourself.

For example, if you are often unable to say yes to invitations from your friends and family because you feel you always have to put yourself last in order to satisfy others, then this might be a sign that you need to take more time for yourself. Your friends and family may be trying to let you know that they need your support in specific areas of their lives, which is another sign that you are not prioritizing your own needs enough. Taking care of the needs of others is important, but it is also just as important for people to learn how to accept the support of others when they need it.

c. Learn to say "No."

Learning to say "No" is a skill many people struggle to perfect, but it is a very important skill to maintain healthy self-esteem and a well-balanced life. Many struggle with this very important concept because they don't want to hurt others by not being able to help them, even if it's for their own good.

It's crucial to develop the ability to say "No" to situations without feeling guilty or acting rude to other people. Learning how to do this can often be helped by asking and listening to the opinions and advice of others, as they may have years of experience and wisdom on how to deal with different situations. Listening to what others have experienced in their lives will also help you recognize when it is appropriate for you to say "No" and when it is not.

How to say "No"

Step 1: Ask yourself, "Is it a moral dilemma?"

There are different kinds of moral dilemmas; some are easy to deal with, and others can be difficult. Your first step is to ask yourself, "Is it a moral dilemma?"

Step 2: Ask yourself if you need to say "Yes" or "No"

Before you say either "Yes" or "No," you have to ask yourself if you really need the favor. You may need your friend's help, but saying yes will cause more problems than it'll solve, or your boss may want you to work extra hours at the office, but going over there will cause more problems than it'll solve.

Step 3: Ask yourself if you can say "No" without hurting the other person's feelings.

I may ask you to run an errand for me, but if it means losing your job or something else important to you, then I can't expect you to do this. Or I may ask for a favor, and you don't want to do it, but doing so will cause me great pain. In this case, it's better for you and me if I accept your refusal than to have to go through the pain of having my request turned down.

Step 4: Ask yourself if there's anything that makes saying "No" difficult.

Do you feel guilty about saying "No" to someone? Or are you afraid of what will happen if you say "No" to the person? If so, learn to deal with those feelings and how to say "No" in a way that doesn't hurt them.

All situations are different, and the differences can vary from person to person, so it's important for everyone to learn how to apply this in every situation. This can be very helpful as it'll help you recognize when your judgment is clouded.

Step 5: Ask yourself who needs your help more than the other person.

Sometimes, helping another person won't solve their dilemma or even make it better at all. In this case, the person you are helping may not appreciate what you are doing for them, and they may feel guilty about it. You can help that person more by helping someone else who needs your help significantly more than the first person does.

d. Involve yourself in different activities.

Getting out and doing things can help you to build your self-esteem. Try to schedule even a small amount of time for activities that you enjoy and that boost your self-esteem.

You can expand your social circle by getting involved in different activities. You could volunteer, join a sports team, or attend a church group. You'll feel better about yourself and be less likely to worry about problems if you are having fun. When something is causing you stress or making you unhappy, try to distract yourself by focusing on something good in your life or something that gives you pleasure; this will help to reinforce the positive aspects of life and encourage self-confidence.

e. Stay away from places, situations, or people that make you unhappy.

Sometimes, the problems we face are caused by how we handle things and situations. It will help if you try to avoid the situations or people that are making you unhappy to ensure that you don't become unhappier as a result.

If it's a person making you unhappy, it will be much worse if you go back to them and speak to them about their behavior. Suppose it's a situation and something is causing problems with your health, education, or relationships. In that case, it makes sense to focus on other aspects of your life rather than prolonging a stressful situation.

Self-confidence is very important in life because it can help you deal with difficult situations, especially when you have an anxious preoccupied attachment. Your ability to overcome insecurities, maintain a positive outlook on life, and be the best version of yourself depends on your level of self-confidence.

It is important to remember that confidence and arrogance are two different things. Arrogance is defined as excessive pride in oneself and one's abilities that interferes with the individual's ability to be viewed favorably by others. Confidence, on the other hand, is self-assurance or belief in one's own abilities.

CHAPTER 11

ENVISIONING THE FUTURE

As stated in the previous chapters, your attachment style can change. It all depends on you and your willingness to change it. Having a secure attachment is possible, and if you want to try to achieve it, you should know that it won't happen overnight. It takes time and patience, but it is possible.

You will show the traits of someone with a secure attachment style in the future without noticing it. This change may not seem to be in your best interest, but it is.

THE TRAITS OF SOMEONE WITH A SECURE ATTACHMENT STYLE

The following are some of the traits that you can possibly start showing in your future:

1. Openly Express Your Feelings

You will feel comfortable expressing your feelings and communicating how you truly feel. You do not hide your preferences or succumb to the pressure of others to conform to their thoughts, beliefs, or desires.

In addition, you will not feel ashamed of yourself and can face any challenges that may come your way. You will not be afraid to speak your mind or confront someone who is being rude or inappropriate.

You will not need someone to validate you or "make you" feel good at all times. You trust your own values, opinions, and self-acceptance. Even if those around you disagree with you or don't want the same things that you do, you won't be afraid to voice your opinions or stand up for what you believe in. You will know when something is valuable and worth saving and when it is just frivolous or not worth the effort. This is a sign that your mind is developing the skills necessary for maintaining a happy and healthy mental well-being in the future.

For example...

In a relationship, you will not be afraid to speak up and voice your opinions, even if it contradicts your partner's thoughts. You can agree to disagree and still have a healthy and positive relationship. You are not afraid of letting others know how you really feel about things or what you want or need from them. You do not feel the burden of keeping it inside; rather, you can share your feelings openly and comfortably with others.

In the workplace, you will feel free to disagree with others or voice your opinion regarding a work matter. You can dare to voice your thoughts and ideas without being afraid of rejection or even getting fired. You can give constructive criticism without hurting others' feelings since you do not care what they think about you and your impression of them. This is because you are confident and secure in who you are as a person, allowing you to grow in terms of relationships and contributions to the workplace.

These situations are hard to handle, but you will understand how to resolve challenges and conflicts in your daily life without getting overly stressed or angry.

2. Trust Others

You will be able to trust others. You will not feel unsafe, threatened, or anxious around unfamiliar people. Even people you do not know very well will make you feel secure and offer a sense of comfort, knowing everything will be okay. You will also not feel uncomfortable when you are around new people or meeting new people because you are comfortable with yourself and the world around you.

You can also trust that others will only come after you if they like the fact that your goals are different from theirs, especially if your goals are for the betterment of everyone. You are confident in your ability to keep everyone safe and to have faith in others to do what is right, despite the fact that this may involve different values and ideas.

For example...

In a relationship, you will feel comfortable and open to sharing your needs with your partner and will not feel uncomfortable if you receive demands from them. You will not be afraid that they can take advantage of you or that they will become possessive of the relationship since this is not a problem in your mind. You can trust that their motives for sharing information with you are solely out of concern for your well-being and that they care about you as a person and want what is best for you rather than playing games or getting revenge on you.

In the workplace, you can trust others and respect their opinions and ideas. You can align with them rather than try to persuade or sway them into being on your side, knowing that they will come around if you truly have the best interest of all parties at heart. You can feel confident about yourself, knowing that you are working for a good cause and doing what is right for everyone involved.

These situations are now possible because you have learned to respect people and are no longer afraid of what they will think or say about you. You are aware of the environment and situation, making it easier to find a solution that satisfies everyone's needs.

3. Independent

You will feel independent. You can be on your own without fear, without feeling insecure, and without feeling like you are not enough for the world. You will not feel alone in this world if you do not want to and will be able to seek help when needed.

You will not rely on others' opinions or judgments. You can look at things from your own perspective and see things in their best light or the truth of a situation. You are not dependent on someone or something outside yourself to make you feel loved or accepted. You can see the positive in everything and everyone without needing anyone's approval. You can be your own person and focus on what you can do in this life, being happy with yourself and what you have.

For example...

You will not feel uncertain or afraid to be alone in a relationship. Because of your self-esteem and confidence, you are comfortable being alone and can go out into the world if you so wish. You do not depend on another person to make you feel better or safe when away from them.

In the workplace, you can tell who is a good fit for the job they have been assigned. You will find yourself more than capable and can focus on what matters in that area more than anything else.

These situations are now possible because you have grown more self-aware and confident in yourself and the world around you. You can respect others and their ideas, even if they differ from yours. You can trust people because of your open-mindedness and willingness to listen without judgment or distraction from other thoughts that might cloud what is really important.

4. Develop Self-Regulation

You will have the ability to develop the skills necessary for maintaining a happy, healthy lifestyle and for coping appropriately with stressful situations. This includes knowing how to deal with problems and stressors in your daily life, such as being upset by someone's behavior or failing something at school.

You can make decisions without feeling overwhelmed with excessive anxiety. You have a healthy mind, which allows you to accept responsibility for your actions and own your mistakes while also having the ability to share this accountability with other people. You can also do this without feeling ashamed of yourself or embarrassed and worried about others' perceptions of you.

For example...

You will have a solid understanding of communication and conflict resolution in relationships. You will be able to manage your emotions rather than stress about the issue or become upset at others for not responding in the way you expect. You can observe what is happening, listen to others, and decide on a course of action. You will not feel overwhelmed or lost when dealing with various relationship issues like disagreements over expectations of each other's actions. In general, you will have great confidence in your relationships and be able to accept everything as it is coming from the other person's perspective.

In the workplace, you will be able to maintain composure, so you are not easily frustrated when faced with a challenge. You will be able to turn away from negative comments, which can cause stress and anxiety, as opposed to resolving the issue at hand. You can also maintain your composure during conflicts, disagreements, or arguments, even when someone speaks in a way you do not like.

These situations are hard to handle, but you will be confident in your ability to deal with them without getting emotionally involved and turning into an emotional mess like you were before.

5. Balanced and in control

You will have an overall feeling of balance and control over your life. You can maximize your time, be productive, and feel peaceful instead of anxious, stressed, or overwhelmed. You do not get overwhelmed easily, and you can easily stay focused on what is happening around you and in the present.

You can set boundaries for yourself, allowing you to control what is happening in your life. This includes understanding your needs, wants, and values and respecting others' needs, wants, and values. Instead of attempting to alter or shape other people into what you want them to be, you can accept them for who they are.

For example...

In relationships, you will not feel the need to control people's actions and emotions by being spiteful or abusive. You will not feel like you are always in power or control, but instead, recognize that each relationship is different and may require different tools to manage. You can accept everyone for who they are because you are confident they have the best intentions for your relationship.

In the workplace, your self-control will allow you to complete tasks on time and put your energy into what needs to be done rather than getting distracted by other things around you. You will be able to set aside time for yourself and ignore any distractions that might try to get in the way of your work or focus.

These situations are possible because you have developed your ability to control emotions and accept things as they happen. You can set aside time for yourself and use this time to accomplish your goals.

6. Mature, Realistic, and Responsible

You'll be in a position to view your life and yourself objectively. You can set realistic goals and make decisions that are best for everyone involved. You can make choices based on what is most important or relevant rather than on your feelings of fear, anger, or guilt because you are not a slave to your emotions. You will be able to prioritize these emotions so they don't distract you from what is happening in the moment or in your life right now.

You will feel confident about your past and be reassured of your future. With a realistic understanding of how things operate, you will be able to view the world around you and base your decisions on it. You are able to ask questions rather than letting people's expectations or explanations create false hopes or expectations in your mind.

For example...

In relationships, you have a good understanding of what you want and need as well as knowing what others want and need. You can become aware of other people's needs, wants, and values without feeling that they are too different from yours or contradicting them. You don't feel the need to force these needs on others or make them change to be in line with what you think is best.

In the workplace, you will clearly understand the goals set out by your company. You can work towards these goals while being realistic and not feeling disappointed if they don't go as planned. You can make decisions based on what is best in a particular situation rather than acting out of anger, revenge, or other negative emotions.

These situations are possible because you understand the world around you well. You can make decisions based on what is happening rather than using other people's expectations or ideas that do not fully back up the facts.

There are numerous things to look forward to in the future. You will be able to live a happy and satisfying life without fear of being controlled by your emotions. You will be able to live the life you've always desired and utilize your gifts. Developing these skills may take some time, but they will be worth it in the end.

CONCLUSION

Attachment is a biologically ingrained mechanism that facilitates the infant's need for caretaking, comfort, and protection. It is one of the most important drives in human life, but its importance doesn't end with childhood.

Anxious preoccupied attachment is an insecure form of attachment characterized by a high level of preoccupation with the availability and safety of the attachment figure, as well as feeling uncomfortable in situations where there is no physical proximity to said figure. This type of attachment is typically found in individuals raised in environments where they were neglected or abused by their caregivers. The parent that was not abusive may have been physically close but emotionally distant, which put pressure on the other parent to meet all needs.

As they age, these children may continue to feel pressure to meet their own needs and those of others, and they are more likely to experience marital dissatisfaction because they may be unable to meet their partner's needs. They tend to have problems with intimacy, commitment, and closeness in relationships and are very uncomfortable with intense emotions, especially anger. These individuals would rather avoid these situations than deal with them head-on. They are insecure in relationships and do not seek help for personal problems. This can cause many problems in their relationships over the long term. They may experience more depression and anxiety.

In their workplace, these individuals are known for having an immense interest in their jobs and a love of rules and order. They are skilled at their jobs and may even possess a high level of proficiency. However, they could be better at taking criticism because they put a great deal of pressure on themselves. They may be hardworking but also play out their own distress on others by being emotionally demanding, critical, or rejecting them.

All of these are typical traits of these individuals, and the possibility of you having this type of attachment style is high. But there is nothing to worry about as your attachment style can change, and you can learn to function better with others. You can do this by knowing and managing your triggers and how to cope with those situations. You can also improve your self-confidence, which can help you feel comfortable in different situations and learn to deal with them more constructively. This can also help you feel comfortable with your own emotions and how to deal with them healthily.

Your future, wherein you can show the traits of someone with secure attachment, is bright. The key is making an effort to change and learning to improve your relationships over time. This will give you a new lease on life and allow you to appreciate the emotional connection between people. You can become the star in your own life, so shine on!

Printed in the USA
CPSIA information can be obtained
at www.ICGtesting.com
LVHW011026241123
764814LV00048B/671